THE APOCALYPSE, RIGHTLY DIVIDING THE REVELATION

The Chronological Order of Events Made Easy

MIKE SANCHEZ

Cover and Interior Design: Derinda Babcock

PUBLISHED BY: Mike Sanchez

Library Cataloging Data

Names: Sanchez, Mike (Mike Sanchez)

The Apocalypse, Rightly Dividing the Revelation: The Chronological Order of Events Made Easy / Mike Sanchez

152 p., 23cm × 15cm (9 in × 6 in.)

Identifiers: ISBN-13: 978-0-578-76419-1 (paperback) | (ebook)

Key Words: Prophecy, The Book of Revelation, Order of Events, End Times, Apocalypse, Rapture, Tribulation

ACKNOWLEDGMENTS

Though I do not completely agree with the following authors' interpretation of the Book of Revelation, I would like to acknowledge these good Bible teachers.

Hal Lindsay

Charles Capps

Les Feldick

Robert Morris

Perry Stone

Andrew Wommack

And I would like to thank my friend, Derinda Babcock, for her help with this book. She had her work cut out for her. In fact, she is due credit for any success this book may achieve.

PREFACE

I read *The Late Great Planet Earth,* by Hal Lindsey back in 1976, and have been hooked on prophesy and the book of Revelation ever since. *The Apocalypse: Rightly Dividing the Revelation* has taken me twenty years to write but with each attempt I've learned more and had to study what I learned. Because of the time and extensive effort I've invested in understanding the prophecies found in the Book of Revelation, I consider myself knowledgeable about the subject.

A man teaching a Bible study on the Book of Revelation made the statement that he believed the Book of Revelation contained no salvation scripture because John was writing to the "church" and the church is already saved. I about fell out of the pew. I don't know about you but I have heard preachers quote salvation scriptures from the book all my life, and I have read these scriptures for myself for years.

I thought I had the understanding I needed to write an explanation of the prophesies found in the book called The Revelation, but the visions, symbolism, and timeline were impossible for me to explain by following the order of chapter and verse. From my studies, I knew the chronological order of the events described, so I put these in order in this book to help readers better understand these prophesies.

I also clarify many misunderstood words, passages, and symbols, so if you're interested in end time prophesy, the

Book of Revelation, rapture, or rupture, the tribulation and the kingdom to come, you are going to love this book. If you do not have at least a basic understanding of the Bible, this book may not be for you.

INTRODUCTION

Why would I write a book on the Book of Revelation? I don't want to argue the book, but rather share what I have learned in a manner that may help readers better understand the truths found in this book. I want to let the text answer the question is there a rapture? If so, is this catching away a pre-tribulation, mid-tribulation, pre-wrath, or post-tribulation event? Why are these questions important, or are they?

Once you read the scriptures written in the Revelation, these questions will answer themselves. You will find more than one answer, and the answers may surprise you.

The word Revelation comes from the Greek ἀποκάλυψις or apokalysis, meaning disclosure: appearing, coming, lighten, manifestation, to be revealed.

In 2 Timothy 2:15, believers are told to "study to shew thyself approved unto God, a workman that needeth not be ashamed, rightly dividing the word of truth." The phrase, rightly dividing, comes from the Greek ὀρθοτομέω or orthotoméō, and means to proceed by straight paths, to hold a straight course, and is equivalent to do right, to expound correctly.

Without jumping ahead into the Book of Revelation, let's see what other New Testament scriptures say about the catching away or rapture of believers.

From Titus 2:13: Looking for that blessed hope, and the glorious appearing of the great God and our savior, Jesus Christ,

And from 2 Peter 3:3-4: Knowing this first, that there shall come in the last days scoffers, walking after their own lusts, and saying, where is the promise of his coming?

Now from 1 Thessalonians 4:17-18 Then we who are alive and remain shall be caught up together with them in the clouds, to meet the Lord in the air; and so shall we ever be with the Lord. Wherefore comfort one another with these words.

Three things we see in these passages associated with the return of Christ.

First the rapture, or catching away of the church, is called that blessed hope.

Second, the rapture is called the promise.

And **third**, we are told to comfort one another with these words.

What if you do not have a personal relationship with Jesus Christ at his return? From the prophet Amos we read, Woe unto you who desire the day of the Lord! For what good is the day of the Lord for you? The day of the Lord is darkness, and not light. Amos 5:18.

Apparently, Amos was writing to Jews who were ignorant of the scriptures.

To shed some light on the previous passage in Amos let's go to Malachi 4:1 and 5.

> 1 For, behold, the day cometh, that shall burn as an oven; and all the proud, yea, all that do wickedly, shall be stubble: and the day that cometh, shall burn them up, sayeth the Lord of hosts, that it shall leave them neither root nor branch.

> 5 Behold, I will send you Elijah the prophet before the coming of the great and dreadful day of the Lord: (Armageddon)

The general day of the Lord begins in Revelation chapter 7 and ends in chapter 22, but there is a specific day, that great and dreadful day known as the Battle of Armageddon.

We will study the book of Revelation and see what the book teaches us as we go through. Rather than speculating on the symbolism, we will check the Bible against the Bible.

The word of God is a witness to itself; many prophets wrote concerning the end times and we will compare their writing to some degree where relevant.

CHAPTER ONE

John's introduction

Who was John, and why would God have John write this book?

John was an apostle of Jesus Christ. The Greek word for apostle is *apostolos* and means messenger, or he that is sent. He also wrote the Gospel of John, 1 John, 2 John, and 3 John. Some people believe John wrote this book prior to the Roman destruction of the temple in Jerusalem in AD 70, but this is not possible.

The events described in this book can never recur—they are final and everlasting. Most Bible scholars agree that John wrote this book about AD 95.

John is not writing a storybook nor is he writing with colorful language and symbolism for anyone's entertainment. He writes only what he is told to write and what he sees and hears.

I believe the Lord told John to write the book and gave him the visions in The Revelation to make clear his certain return.

The time of mankind's rule over mankind is limited, but God's rule will last forever, and his gift of salvation is free to all who will accept it.

God isn't finished with the Jewish people who rejected their Messiah Jesus. He has set aside a period of time to reveal Jesus again to them who are alive at that time and to all who have rejected his grace.

John also gives a warning of the terrible judgments that will come upon the earth and the eternal judgment of mankind who refuse the righteousness that Jesus purchased on our behalf.

What is the meaning of the letters to the seven churches?

First, I believe the letters are a look into God's love for mankind and his blessing to all who rely on the finished work of Jesus. The letters in the Book of Revelation show his love for his church body, his blessing in this life, and his promise to restore the heavens and earth to their intended glory.

Second, in the letters in the book of Revelation, Jesus warns unbelievers of their need of God's salvation by the shed blood of Jesus alone. For those who do not believe and trust in Jesus, whether or not they attend church, there is no salvation—only eternal separation from God.

In the letters to the seven churches in chapters two and three, Jesus calls the unbelievers to himself through salvation scripture at the end of each of the letters.

There is no need for Jesus to call the saved to salvation. For example, in John 6:37, Jesus said, All that the Father giveth me shall come to me; and him that cometh to me I will in no wise cast out.

He has prepared a place for us, the church, to be with him in heaven where I believe we will be during the tribulation period. He has made a way for 144,000 apostles to preach the gospel during the first half of the tribulation, and he will send his two prophets of old during the second half to work signs and wonders of the Lord God so people might give God glory and be saved.

Revelation 11:7 and 13 says the two prophets will be killed, then after three-and-a-half days, God will raise them.

13 And the same hour was there a great earthquake, and a tenth of the city fell, and in the earthquake were slain of men seven thousand: and the remnant were affrighted and gave glory to the God of heaven.

I have heard teaching in church and statements on Christian TV which for me just do not make sense.

When speaking of the rapture and the opening of the seven seals, the preachers and teachers I've heard regurgitate the same common misunderstanding of the symbolism in Revelation. In some cases, they have an opinion so far from any scriptural interpretation, that I am uncertain how they came up with such bizarre ideas.

Many teach that when John is called up to heaven in Revelation chapter 4, and he sees an open door, somehow that is a picture of the rapture.

John gives an account of exactly who is in the presence of God, and there isn't the presence of the resurrected and raptured saints until chapter 7.

When Jesus opens the first seal in chapter 6:1-2, a white horse appears and the rider has a bow and is given a crown. This is not a symbol of the coming antichrist as many teach.

From the writers of other books in the Bible, the Bible shows us who the horsemen are and what the horses represent.

The seven seals are not seven separate and individual judgments. I give examples in this book.

I have laid out the Book of Revelation in chronological order which makes passages a lot easier to understand and lays out the timeline, the prophetic scenes, and symbolism in the book.

Many prophesies have been fulfilled in Israel over the past century, so I believe we are in the last days, and that the events of the Book of Revelation are about to be fulfilled.

I have an almost overwhelming desire for people to know the truth of the prophesy in the book of Revelation.

You will have a better understanding of your relationship with the Lord and a much clearer picture of the Revelation if you read this book. Reading prophesy is a little like watching a movie or reading a novel; the characters in the scene are going about their daily lives, then they have a flashback of an earlier time or dreams of a future event.

The Book of Revelation, the Bible prophesy does not read top left to bottom right by chapter and verse. Prophecy must be interpreted in the context of the text.

In the book of Revelation, the many references to three-and-a-half years, forty-two months, one thousand two hundred sixty days, or a time, times and a half a time, gives a specific mid-tribulation timeline. This timeline will guide us through the book.

My intention is to make the book that John wrote easier to understand with few references or comments. I hope this works for you.

I have emphasized certain words, phrases, and symbols with the intent that these emphases will make your reading easier.

My comments on the text are not as important as your reading of the text in context.

Who was Melchisedec? Many teach that Melchizedek was Shem or perhaps a Canaanite king who was both King and priest, but in context of the text he is Jesus.

Hebrews 7:1-3: For this Melchisedec, king of Salem, priest of the most high God … first being by interpretation King of righteousness, and after that also King of Salem, which is King of peace;

Without father, without mother, without descent, having neither beginning of days, nor end of life; but made like unto the Son of God; abideth a priest continually.

This scripture is a good example of context, see also Psalm 110.

This man is not a mortal man the text says that he is without ancestry, that rules out a man.

Melchizedek is first by interpretation King of righteousness with a capitol K as in King of kings.

And after that, he is King of peace, priest of the most high God, made like unto the Son of God, and lives as a priest forever.

And he isn't an angel. The Lord appeared to Abraham in Genesis 18, he wrestled with Jacob in chapter 32:24-32, in verse 30 Jacob said of the man he wrestled with, I have seen God face to face, and my life is preserved.

How about Daniel's buddies in Daniel 3:25? He answered and said, Lo, I see four men loose walking in the midst of the fire, … and the form of the fourth is like the son of God.

Notice he said the form of the man looks like the Son of God. The king knew what he was seeing, so he called to the three servants of the most high God, come here.

When God Almighty appeared to men as a man, he was Jesus. Ephesians 3:9

Revelation Chapter One

> 1 The Revelation of Jesus Christ, which God gave unto Him, (Jesus) to shew unto His servants things which must shortly come to pass; and He (God) sent and signified it by his angel (messenger, Jesus) unto his servant John:
>
> 2 Who bore record (witness) of the word of God, and of the testimony of Jesus Christ, and of all things that he (John) saw.
>
> 3 Blessed is he that readeth, and they that hear the words of this prophesy, and keep those things which are written therein: for the time is at hand.

No other book in the Bible starts off with a blessing like this. The blessing is repeated in Chapter 22:7-8: "Behold, I come quickly: blessed is he that keepeth the sayings of the prophesy of this book."

This book is meant to be understood. Jesus just said so. And he said in Matthew 10:26 and Mark 4:22, there is nothing hidden that shall not be known, etc.

Then the book ends with a curse in Chapter 22:18-19.

> 18 For I (Jesus) testify unto every man that heareth the words of the prophesy of this book, If, any man shall add unto these things, God shall add unto him the plagues that are written in this book:
>
> 19 And if any man shall take away from the words of the book of this prophesy, God shall take away his part out of the book of life, and out of the holy city, and from the things which are written in this book.

Continuing with Revelation Chapter One

> 4 John, to the seven churches (assemblies, congregations, synagogues) which are in Asia: Grace be unto you, and peace, from him which is, and which was, and which is to come; and from the seven Spirits which are before his throne.

The seven spirits before the throne here are the attributes of the Holy Spirit as described in Isaiah 11:2: And the Spirit of the Lord shall rest upon him (Jesus), the spirit of wisdom and understanding, the spirit of counsel and might, the spirit of knowledge and the fear of the Lord;

> 5 And from Jesus Christ, who is the faithful witness, and the first begotten (born, raised) of the dead, (Acts 13:33-34) and the prince of the kings of the earth. Unto him that loved us and washed us from our sins in his own blood, (not water)

> 6 And hath made us kings and priests unto God his Father; to him be glory and dominion forever and ever. Amen.

> 7 Behold he cometh with clouds; (saints) and every eye shall see him, and they also which pierced him: and all kindreds of the earth shall wail because of him. Even so, Amen.

Jude 1:14 ... Behold the Lord cometh with ten thousands of his saints,

This event happens at the battle of Armageddon Revelation chapter 16, and we know from Revelation 19:14 that the armies which are in heaven follow him upon white horses clothed in fine linen white and clean. Therefore from the context I believe the clouds here represent the saints and angels.

A prophetic scene described in Matthew 24:30-31 supports this idea.

> 30 And then shall appear the sign of the Son of man in heaven; (sky) and then shall the tribes of the earth mourn, and they shall see the Son of man coming in the clouds of heaven with power and great glory.

A cloud represents the power and glory of God, but in Rev. 1:7 and Matt. 24:30 he comes in or with the clouds, plural.

> 31 And he shall send his angels with a great sound of a trumpet, and they shall gather his elect (the saints) from the four winds, from one end of heaven to the other. (Daniel 7:13)

The saints of God share and reflect his glory, Luke 9:29-31 the appearance of Jesus changed and his clothes were white and glistening, and Moses and Elijah appeared in glory.

Verses 34 and 35 … there came a cloud, and over shadowed them; and they feared as they entered into the cloud.

And there came a voice out of the cloud, …

The kings and the nations shall bring "their glory" into the holy city, the new Jerusalem, Rev. 21:24-26.

Paul writes of a cloud as the saints in Hebrews 11, the heroes of the faith the saints that went before us.

Then in chapter 12:1 wherefore seeing we also are compassed about with so great a cloud of witnesses, ...

Isaiah 14:14 I (Satan) will ascend above the heights of the clouds; I will be like the most High. 15 Yet thou shalt be brought down to hell, … Are these physical clouds?

Isaiah 14:12 and 13 helps give us the context of the text, How art thou fallen from heaven, O Lucifer, … 13 For thou hast said in thy heart, I will ascend into heaven, I will exalt my throne above the stars (angels) of God: I will sit also upon the mount of the congregation, …

The mount or mountain is the kingdom of God or the seat of his power and is above the congregation of saints in heaven.

The word nephos, translated cloud in Hebrews 12:1, denotes a cloudy, shapeless mass covering the heavens. Hence, metaphorically, of a dense multitude, a throng.

Another word translated cloud, most often in the New Testament is the word nephele, a definitely shaped cloud, or masses of clouds possessing definite form.

This word is used metaphorically to speak of evil people in 2 Peter 2:17

> These are wells without water, clouds that are carried with a tempest: to whom the mist of darkness is reserved forever.

Throughout the book of Revelation, the word cloud does not refer to a naturally occurring cloud.

Our heavenly Father speaks to us all, not by words that we hear with our ears but by an unction, a moving in the spirit and through his written word.

A good Bible dictionary and lexicon is an essential tool in the study of the Bible but the simple definition of a word doesn't by itself-give us the spiritual interpretation found in the context of scripture.

Continuing Revelation Chapter One

> 8 I am Alpha and Omega, the beginning, and the ending, sayeth the Lord God, who is, and which was, and which is to come, the Almighty.

> 9 I John, who also am your brother, and companion in tribulation, (the persecution of the church) and in the Kingdom and patience of Jesus Christ, was in the Isle

that is called Patmos, for the word of God, and for the testimony of Jesus Christ.

10 I was in the Spirit on the Lord's day, and heard behind me a great voice, as of a trumpet,

John has, so far, written symbolically of God the Father and Jesus, God the Son, as separate or individual personalities, but now Jesus begins to speak directly to John in Revelation 1:11

11 Saying, I am Alpha and Omega, the first and the last: and, What thou seest write in a book, and send it to the seven churches (assemblies) which are in Asia: Unto Eph'e-sus, and unto Smyrna, and unto Per'ga-mos, and unto Thy-ati'ra, and unto Sardis, and unto Philadelphia, and unto La-od-i-ce'a.

12 And I turned to see the voice that spake with me. And being turned, I saw seven golden candlesticks;

13 And in the midst the seven candlesticks one like unto the Son of man, clothed with a garment down to the foot, and girt about the paps with a golden girdle. (vest)

14 His head and his hairs were white like wool, as white as snow; and his eyes were like a flame of fire.

15 And his feet like unto fine brass, as if they burned (refined) in a furnace; and his voice as the sound of many waters.

16 And he had in his right hand seven stars: and out of his mouth went a sharp twoedged sword: and his countenance was as the sun shineth in his strength. (Malachi 4:2)

17 And when I saw him, I fell at his feet as dead. And he laid his right hand upon me saying unto me, Fear not; I am the first and the last:

18 I am he that liveth, and was dead; and, behold, I am alive for evermore, Amen: and have the keys of hell and of death.

In the previous eight verses, we see Jesus in the fullness of the Father, Son and Holy Spirit, and now he will personally dictate these letters to John.

19 Write the things which thou hast seen, (just now) and the things which are, (chapters 2 and 3) and the things which shall be hereafter;

20 The mystery of the seven stars which thou sawest in my right hand, and the seven golden candlesticks. The seven stars are the seven angels (messengers, pastors) of the seven churches (assemblies): and the seven lampstands which thou sawest are the seven churches. (assemblies, gathering places)

We must address this mystery of the seven stars and the seven candlesticks. Jesus explains them to John, but the translation is lacking.

Vine's Expository Dictionary of Biblical Words, the English word angel is related to the Greek word *angelos*, whose translation is similar to the Hebrew: "messenger" or angel.

Angel should be translated and understood as messenger, the pastor or preacher in this instance, and the word translated "churches" should be understood as the "assembly" or where the congregation meets. The church is the body of Christ as depicted in the following scriptures.

> Matthew 16:18, Jesus said, "I will build my church; and the gates of hell shall not prevail against it."

He was not speaking of a building made with hands.

And in 18:17 "tell it unto the church: but if he neglect to hear the church ..."

You wouldn't have a conversation with a building would you?

Acts 2:47 "And the Lord added to the church daily such as should be saved."

In Ephesians 5:23-32 we see that the church is the body of true believers.

> 23 Christ is the head of the church: and he is the saviour of the body.
>
> 25 Christ also loved the church, and gave himself for it;
>
> 26 That he might sanctify and cleanse it with the washing of water by the word,
>
> 29 For no man ever yet hated his own flesh; but nourisheth and cherisheth it, even as the Lord the church:
>
> 30 For we are members of his body, of his flesh, and of his bones.
>
> 32 This is a great mystery: but I speak concerning Christ and the church.

Let's look at the definition of candlestick in the context of the text, the lampstands are the seven assemblies.

Vine's Expository Dictionary of Biblical Words, the word *luchnia* is mistranslated "candlestick" in every occurrence in the King James Version (KJV).

Jesus explains in Revelation 1:20:

> The mystery of the seven stars which thou sawest in my right hand, and the seven golden candlesticks.
>
> The seven stars are the seven angels (pastors) of the seven churches; (assemblies) and the seven candlesticks (lampstands) which thou sawest are the seven churches. (assemblies)

Look up the word translated church. You are referred to the word assembly and congregation. The word *ekklesia* was used by the Greeks of a body of citizens "gathered" to discuss the affairs of state.

In the Septuagint, the word is used to designate the "gathering" of Israel, summoned for any definite purpose.

This gathering has two applications to companies of Christians, (a) to the whole company of the redeemed throughout the present era, as I previously quoted from Matthew 16:18, and Ephesians 5:23-32, and (b) in the singular as I quoted from Matthew 18:17.

King James insisted that the English translation use the word church rather than assembly which, in my opinion, was a poison dart aimed directly to the heart of Christendom.

In my experience, I have never heard there were unbelievers in any of the seven assemblies in the book of Revelation, but rather that the letters are written to the "church."

This idea seems to be almost universal, and if we believe Jesus is threatening us the church, the body and bride of Christ saying that you, the church have a reputation of being alive but in fact you are dead, we will have a tainted view of our relationship with him.

Jesus is not speaking to the "church" when he says that he will cast her into a bed and those who commit adultery with her into great tribulation and kill her children with death.

This idea that Jesus is rebuking the "church" effects our confidence and or our opinion of others.

How many times have you heard a pastor call for an alter call either as a call to salvation or as a rededication to the Lord?

I have attended a small congregation were this was a weekly occurrence, even though the pastor new everyone in attendance.

I was unfriended by a Facebook friend that thought only water baptism saves, and that the song *Saved by the Blood* was blasphemy. He called me a heretic.

I have been unfriended by relatives, because I believe that Jesus still heals. They say that healing was from a different dispensation. Show me the dispensation that divides the church age.

In my opinion, people are quick to accept whatever sounds good to them at the time, and they hang on to their beliefs because they won't study the word for themselves. I hope we end that practice here and now.

CHAPTER 2

John writes to the seven assemblies

We know from Revelation chapter 1:3, that everyone who reads or hears the prophesy of this book is blessed if they take the words to heart, so this entire book would have been delivered to the seven assemblies.

Jesus now dictates to John these seven letters to the assemblies with a specific message to each, but the message is timeless and universal.

All the people in the assembly at Ephesus are the church and are saved, born again believers.

Some scholars, even some Bible translations, refer to this assembly as the loveless church. One translation even says that they have left Jesus. This idea is wrong.

What does the text say? To the assembly in Ephesus John wrote in chapter 2:2 and 3

> 2 I know thy works, and thy labour, and thy patience, ...

> 3 And hast borne, and hast patience, and for my name's sake hast labored, and hast not fainted.

This is not a loveless church. They have lost the joy of the *agape*, God kind of love that they had at first, and this is probably the result of enduring hardship, or perhaps, they have lost sight of God's love for them.

Pastor John Hagee taught on TV about the love of God and how a Christian can love like God. Loving is to forgive as Jesus forgave us.

And we should forgive ourselves as well as others. My takeaway from his message is that forgiveness is the practical application of God's love.

The church in Ephesus have not grown weary of Jesus; they have not grown weary of doing good, and they are not without natural love.

A lot of people teach and preach that Jesus is chastising the church in these seven letters. They say that the churches have not remained faithful for the most part.

That is just not true according to Paul. The Lord remains faithful. 2 Timothy 2:13: If we believe not, yet he abideth faithful: he cannot deny himself.

What does "he cannot deny himself" mean? If you are in Christ, he is in you, so he cannot deny himself, because we are one body.

2 Timothy 2:15: Study to shew thyself approved unto God, a workman that needeth not to be ashamed, rightly dividing the word of truth.

Revelation Chapter Two

> 1 Unto the angel (pastor) of the church (assembly) in Eph'e-sus write; These things saith he that holdeth the seven stars (pastors) in his right hand, who walketh in the midst of the seven golden candlesticks; (assemblies)

Jesus calls them golden assemblies, because they were founded in the name of the Lord Jesus Christ, and, as Paul wrote to the Ephesians around thirty years earlier, they have been around for a while.

> 2 I know thy works, and thy labour, and thy patience, and how thou canst not bear them which are evil: and thou hast tried them which say that they are apostles, and are not, and hast found them liars:
>
> 3 And hast borne, and hast patience, and for my name's sake hast labored, and hast not fainted.
>
> 4 Nevertheless I have somewhat against thee, because thou hast left thy first love.

The love you had at first—please note that John is writing to the pastor, not necessarily the whole congregation, although the message may pertain to all or part of the congregation.

In Ephesians 1:15 Paul wrote, Wherefore I also, after I heard of your faith in the lord Jesus, and love unto all the saints, ... This maybe their first love or the love they had at first.

> 5 Remember therefore from whence thou art fallen, and repent, and do the works; or else I will come unto thee quickly, and will remove thy candlestick out of his place, except thou repent.

He will remove your 'candlestick,' gathering place, from his place not the star or pastor and not the church or body of Christ.

> 6 But this thou hast, that thou hatest the deeds of the Nicolaitans, which I also hate.

Next comes salvation scripture, even though the members of this assembly are saved, born again believers. This book of the Bible and these letters were to be read to the people regardless of whether or not they already have a relationship with the Lord Jesus Christ.

> 7 He that hath an ear, let him hear what the Spirit saith unto the churches; (assemblies) To him that overcometh will I give to eat of the tree of life, which is in the midst of the paradise of God.

"To him that overcomes" … Let's see what this same John had to say about that in 1 John 5:4-5

> 4 For whatsoever is born of God overcometh the world: and this is the victory that overcometh the world, even our faith.

> 5 Who is he that overcometh the world, but he that believeth that Jesus is the Son of God?

Jesus does not have one criticism of the church in the assembly in Smyrna.

> 2:8 And unto the angel (pastor) of the church (assembly) in Smyrna write; These things saith the first and the last, which was dead, and is alive;

> 9 I know thy works, and tribulation, and poverty, but thou art rich (I have nothing against you) and I know the blasphemy of them which say they are Jews, and are not, but are the synagogue (assembly) of Satan.

> 10 Fear none of those things which thou shalt suffer: behold, the devil shall cast some of you in prison, that ye may be tried; and ye shall have tribulation ten days: be thou faithful unto death, and I will give thee a crown of life.

Jesus warns these believers that some of them will be put in prison and this persecution will last ten days, he doesn't say that some would be put to death, we have implied that.

Now for the salvation scripture.

> 11 He that hath an ear, let him hear what the Spirit saith to the churches: (assemblies)
>
> He that overcometh shall not be hurt of the second death.

Once again let's see what John has to say about overcoming from 1 John 2:12-14

> 12 ... your sins are forgiven you for his name's sake.
>
> 13 ...ye have overcome the evil one.
>
> 14 ... and the word of God (Jesus) abideth in you, and ye have overcome the evil one.

The church, the true believers in Pergamos have a couple of problems they have some people there that go to the assembly but they are not the church, not the body of Christ.

Continuing Revelation Two

> 12 To the angel (pastor) of the church (assembly) in Per'ga-mos write; These things saith he which hath the sharp sword with two edges;
>
> 13 I know thy works, and where thou dwellest, even where Satan's seat is: and thou holdest fast my name, and hast not denied my faith, even in those days

> wherein An'ti-pas was my faithful martyr, (witness) who was slain among you, where Satan dwelleth.

> 14 But, I have a few things against thee, because thou hast there them that hold the doctrine of Balaam, (Numbers 31:16) who taught Balak to put a stumblingblock before the children of Israel, to eat things sacrificed unto idols, and to commit fornication.

Jude 8 through 16 describes people who hold to this doctrine.

> 15 So hast thou also them that hold to the doctrine of the Nicolaitans, which thing I hate.

3 John:9-11 describes those who hold to this doctrine.

These two doctrines are essentially the same. Read all of 2 Peter 2 with the understanding that the people described are not backslidden or apostate Christians as some teach. (Luke 8:4-15)

Jesus told John to write to the pastors but there may be other believers in the congregation that are tolerant of those who are proud and hold to a doctrine of greed, personal gain, and betrayal so the church as a whole is responsible to correct this.

Notice that Jesus hates the doctrines of Balaam and Nicolas, but he doesn't hate them.

> 2:16 Repent; or else I will come unto thee quickly, and will fight against them with the sword of my mouth.

Jesus loves his church and doesn't condemn the church. He condemns only those who would corrupt his body.

Those who hold to the teachings of the Nicolaitans and Balaam are not born-again believers, and Jesus speaks of them saying, I will fight against them with the sword of my mouth.

Even though Balaam was a prophet, he was willing to sell out his own people for personal gain. Likewise, Nicol followed after the same spirit. There are some here that need salvation scripture.

Speaking of such people, John wrote concerning imposters in 1 John 2:18-19:

> 18 Little children, it is the last time: and as ye have heard that antichrist shall come, even now are there many antichrists; whereby we know that it is the last time.

> 19 They went out from us, but they were not of us, for if they had been of us, they would no doubt have continued with us: but they went out, that they might be made manifest that they were not all of us.

Back to Revelation Two

Salvation scripture

> 17 He that hath an ear, let him hear what the Spirit says to the churches; (assemblies) To him that overcometh, I will give to eat of the hidden manna, and will give him a white stone, and in the stone a new name written, which no one knoweth except him who receives it.

The church in Thyatira has a problem. They have an evil, wicked woman there who is of the devil. She is not a believer in the risen Lord.

> 18 And unto the angel (pastor) of the church (assembly) in Thyatira write; These things saith the Son of God, who hath his eyes like unto a flame of fire, and his feet are like fine brass;

> 19 I know thy works, and charity, and service, and faith, and thy patience, and thy works; and the last to

be more than the first.

20 Notwithstanding I have a few things against thee, because thou sufferest (allows) that woman Jezebel, which calleth herself a prophetess, to teach and to seduce my servants to commit (spiritual) fornication, and to eat things sacrificed unto idols.

21 And I gave her space to repent of her fornication; and she repented not.

22 Behold, I will cast her into a bed, and them that commit adultery (worship false gods) with her into great tribulation, except they repent of their deeds.

23 And I will kill her children with death; and all the churches (assemblies) shall know that I am he which searcheth the reins and hearts: and I will give unto every one of you according to your works.

By your confession of faith In the Lord and his finished work, or by rejecting him and his saving grace, these are your works.

Her children would be those who are not just misled, but are those who hold to her teaching, her spiritual followers.

24 But unto you I say, and unto the rest in Thy-a-ti'ra, as many as have not this doctrine, and which have not known the depths of Satan, as they speak; I will put upon you none other burden.

25 But that which ye have already hold fast till I come.

The true church or body of believers are not admonished here but only those who hold to these false pagan teachings, and apparently, she is the only one in this congregation that knows the depths of Satan and holds to these teachings.

> 26 And he that overcometh, and keepeth my works unto the end, to him I will give power over the nations (all believers are overcomers):

> 27 And he shall rule them with a rod of iron; as the vessels of a potter shall they be broken to shivers: even as I received of my Father.

> 28 And I will give him the morning star. (Jesus, the Sun of righteousness Malachi 4:2)

> 29 He that hath an ear, let him hear what the Spirit saith unto the churches (assemblies).

Let's look at verse 26 for minute, "and does my works to the end." Some translations use the word deeds or will.

What is Jesus's will or deeds or works? The first thing to understand is that God's very nature is love. John 15:12 says, This is my commandment, that ye love one another, as I have loved you.

The loss of focus on God's love for them was the problem with the assembly at Ephesus in the first letter. They had gotten caught up in the hardships and works of this life and drifted away from the love of God, the agape God kind of love for them.

Paul wrote concerning our eternal security and God's love for us in Romans 8:35-39

> 35 Who shall separate us from the love of Christ? shall tribulation, or distress, or persecution, or famine, or nakedness, or peril, or sword?

36 As it is written, For thy sake we are killed all day long; we are accounted as sheep for the slaughter.

37 Nay, (NO!) in all these things we are more than conquerors through him that loved us.

38 For I am persuaded that neither death, nor life, nor angels, nor principalities, nor powers, nor things present, nor things to come,

39 Nor height, nor depth, nor any other creature, shall be able to separate us from the love of God, which is in Christ Jesus, our Lord.

Satan has been trying to divide the true church and has been successful. He has pitted the denominations against one another.

Paul had to address this same issue with the church in Corinth. The problem continues to this day.

1 Corinthians 3:3-4

3 For ye are yet carnal: for whereas there is among you envying, and strife, and divisions, are ye not carnal, and walk as (natural, earthly) men?

4 For while one (of you) saith, I am of (follow) Paul; and another (says) I am of Apollos; are ye not carnal?

We should all obey the law of liberty to love one another and build up the body of Christ rather than tear one another down.

Galatians 5:1 Stand fast therefore in the liberty wherewith Christ hath made us free, and be not entangled again with the yoke of bondage.

You should read the first six verses of chapter five; Jesus

has set the church free from the law.

James 1:25: But whoso looketh into the perfect law of liberty, and continueth therein, he being not a forgetful hearer, but doer of the work, this man shall be blessed in his deed.

James 2:8 If ye fulfil the royal law according to the scripture, Thou shalt love thy neighbor as thy self, ye do well:

Just as there were unbelievers in some of the seven assemblies in Asia, there are unbelievers in some assemblies still. I believe there are believers in all the Christian denominations.

All believers have one thing in common: if we as individuals, not as a denomination or congregation, know, trust, and believe John 3:16-18

> 16 For God so loved the world, that he gave his only begotten Son, that whosoever believeth in him should not perish, but have ever lasting life.
>
> 17 For God sent not his son into the world to condemn the world; but that the world through him might be saved.
>
> 18 He that believeth on him is not condemned: but he that believeth not is condemned already, because he hath not believed in the name of the only begotten Son of God.

Revelation Chapter Three

The letters to the assemblies continue

The church in Sardis has a big problem because there is almost no church here, those who attend consist mostly of nonbelievers.

> 1 And unto the angel (pastor) of the church (assembly) in Sardis write; These things saith he that hath the seven Spirits (attributes of the Holy Spirit) of God, and the seven stars; (pastors) I know thy works, that thou hast a name that thou livest, and art dead.
>
> 2 Be watchful and strengthen the things which remain, that are ready to die: for I have not found thy works perfect before my God.

To better understand these passages let's go to Matthew 13:5-6, Jesus is the sower and the people of the world are the soils. I am just giving you the parts that I believe to be most relevant to some in this congregation.

> 5 Some (seed) fell upon stony places, where they had not much earth: and forthwith (immediately) they sprung up, because they had no deepness of earth:
>
> 6 And when the sun was up, they were scorched; and because they had no root, they withered away.

The word forthwith literally means immediately; without delay.

See what Luke wrote in Luke chapter eight.

> 11 Now the parable is this: the seed is the word of God.
>
> 12 Those by the way side are they that hear; and then cometh the devil, (immediately) and taketh away the word (seed) out of their hearts, lest they should believe and be saved.
>
> 13 They on the rock are they, which, when they hear, receive the word with joy; and these have no root,

which for a while believe, and in time of temptation fall away.

Continuing with Revelation Three

3 Remember therefore how thou hast received and heard, and hold fast, and repent. If therefore thou shalt not watch, I will come on thee as a thief, and thou shalt not know what hour I will come upon thee, (the tribulation)

4 Thou hast (only) a few names even in Sardis which have not defiled their garments; and they shall walk with me, in white: for they are worthy. (by faith in his grace)

Now the salvation scripture,

5 He that overcometh, the same shall be clothed in white raiment; and I will not blot out his name out of the book of life, but will confess his name before my Father, and before his angels.

6 He who has an ear, let him hear what the Spirit saith to the churches (assemblies).

From the previous verse 5, but I will confess his name before my Father ... and not spew them out of his mouth as in Revelation 3:16 and 17.

16 ... So then because thou art lukewarm (indifferent), and neither cold nor hot, I will spue thee out of my mouth.

He will not confess his name as in Revelation 3:5, but his name will be blotted out of the book of life. He can't blot out your name if your name isn't already written in the book of life.

Jesus is speaking salvation scripture to the lost in verse 5, so the lost must have their names written in the book of life to start with.

Most of the people in this congregation are churchgoers only and are not the "church."

I believe your name is written in the book of life, Revelation 17:8 ... and they that dwell on the earth shall wonder, whose names were not written in the book of life from the foundation of the world.

These people who 'wonder' missed the rapture of the church and are in the tribulation because they rejected Jesus.

The church in Philadelphia, as noted earlier, has their religious doctrine in order. All who are in the assembly are born again believers.

Revelation 3 continues

> 7 And to the angel (pastor) of the church (assembly) in Philadelphia write; These things saith he that is holy, and he that is true, he that hath the key of David. He that openeth, and no man shutteth; and shutteth and no man openeth.

> 8 I know thy works: (I have nothing against you) behold, I have set before thee an open door, and no man can shut it: for thou hast a little strength, and hast kept my word, and hast not denied my name.

> 9 Behold, I will make them of the synagogue (assembly) of Satan, which say they are Jews, and are not, but do lie; behold, I will make them to come and worship before thy feet, and know that I have loved thee.

> 10 Because thou have kept the word of my patience, I will also keep thee from the hour (time) of temptation, (tribulation) which shall come upon all the world, to try them that dwell upon the earth.

The congregation in Philadelphia will not be living here on earth, but a type of this congregation will be.

The "hour of trial" is the seven-year tribulation period which will follow in this book of prophesy, this seven-year period is prophesied in Daniel 9:27.

And he (antichrist) shall confirm the covenant with many (nations) for one week (of years): and in the midst of the week (3.5 years) he shall cause the sacrifice and the oblation to cease …

Now the salvation scripture Revelation 3

> 11 Behold, I come quickly: hold that fast which thou hast, that no man take thy crown.

> 12 Him that overcometh will I make a pillar in the temple of my God, and he shall go no more out: and I will write upon him the name of my God, and the name of the city of my God, which is new Jerusalem, which cometh down out of heaven from my God: and I will write upon him my new name.

> 13 He that hath an ear, let him hear what the Spirit saith to the churches (assemblies).

Not one individual or group in the assembly at Philadelphia is admonished in this letter, yet there is salvation scripture. The name Philadelphia means brotherly love, which is the proper attitude of the true church.

The church in Laodicea does not have a problem, because there is no church there. Those who assemble are self-righteous church goers.

Jesus starts and ends with salvation scripture in this letter because there isn't one Christian in the whole bunch!

> 14 And unto the angel (pastor) of the church (assembly) of the La-od-i-ce'ans write; These things saith the Amen, the faithful and true witness, the beginning of the creation of God;

> 15 I know thy works, that thou art neither cold nor hot: I would thou wert cold or hot.

> 16 So then because thou art lukewarm, and neither cold nor hot, (indifferent) I will spue thee out of my mouth.

Revelation 3:5 I will confess his name ... is the apparent opposite of I will spew you out, or I will not confess your name.

The word spew literally means to vomit or expel. I like what *Thayer's Lexicon* says, "to reject with extreme disgust, Rev. 3:16."

I'm sure you've had a drink of lukewarm water or maybe milk. You may have spit the liquid out, but I doubt you puked with extreme disgust.

Folks, this isn't rocket science. God gave us an imagination and his Holy Spirit. We were created in his image.

This word spue is the apparent opposite of Revelation 3:5. I will confess or speak your name out of my mouth before my God and his holy angels.

The book of Revelation is a book of symbols, but it's not a book of mysteries. Consider the sharp two-edged sword that Jesus has in his mouth.

There is no such thing as a lukewarm church: a person is either in the body of Christ or not.

Would a cold 'Christian' somehow be more desirable to God?

Yes.

Some teachers say that Jesus referred to the term lukewarm because of the tepid water supply in Laodicea and go on to describe the assembly as the lukewarm church. That's ignorant.

Merriam Webster, lukewarm, 2: lacking conviction: ...

Dictionary.com, lukewarm, 2 ... indifferent:

Continuing Chapter Three

> 17 Because thou sayest, I am rich, and increased with goods, and have need of nothing; and knowest not that thou are wretched, and miserable, and poor, and blind and naked:

> 18 I counsel thee to buy of me gold tried in the fire, that thou mayest be rich; and white raiment, that thou mayest be clothed, (gifts of salvation) and that the shame of thy nakedness do not appear; and anoint thine eyes with eyesalve, that thou mayest see.

> 19 As many as I love, I rebuke (teach, correct) and chasten (disciple, train).

Remember John 3:16? For God so loved the world, that he gave his only begotten Son, that whosoever believeth in him shall not perish, but have everlasting life.

Now back to the last verses of Revelation Three

> 20 Behold, I stand at the door and knock: (Jesus is not standing outside of his church, his own body.) If any

> man hear my voice, (word) and open the door, (of his heart) I will come in to him, and will sup with him, and he with me.
>
> 21 To him that overcometh, will I grant to sit with me in my throne, even as I also overcame, and am set down with my Father in his throne.
>
> 22 He that hath an ear, let him hear what the Spirit saith unto the churches (assemblies).

There is not one person in this whole congregation saved, not one except perhaps the pastor, and we could only assume that. This is not the church, this is not the body of believers or the body of Christ.

You can have people who attend an assembly, but who don't know God from a goose.

1 John 2:18-19

> 18 … Even now are there many antichrists; whereby we know that it is the last time.
>
> 19 They went out from us, but they were not of us: for if they had been of us, they would no doubt have continued with us: but they went out, that they might be made manifest that they were not all of us.

The Greek word apostasia, translated apostacy, is only used twice in the New Testament. Once in Acts 21:21, when Paul was falsely accused of teaching Jews to turn away from (the law of) Moses, and the second in 2 Thessalonians 2:3, where Paul explains to the Thessalonians that the (Great and Terrible) "Day of the Lord" is not at hand.

He goes on to explain that there will be "apostasy"—a falling away, when the man of sin is revealed during the mid-tribulation period.

2 Thessalonians 2:1-3:

> 1 Now we beseech you brethren, by the coming of our Lord Jesus Christ, and by our gathering together unto him,
>
> 2 That you be not soon shaken in mind, or be troubled, neither by spirit, nor by word, nor by letter as from us, that the day of Christ is at hand.
>
> 3 Let no man deceive you by any means: for that day shall not come (the day of his wrath), except there comes a falling away first, and (at that time) that man of sin be revealed, the son of perdition (destruction, the antichrist);

True believers will not fall away, because that is impossible based on the previous verses.

Once again, Luke describes these fallen people in Luke 8:11, 12 and 14:

> 11 Now the parable is this: The seed is the word of God.
>
> 12 Those by the way side are they that hear; then cometh the devil, and (forthwith, immediately) taketh away the word out of their hearts, lest they should believe and be saved.
>
> 14 And they which fell among thorns are they, which, when they have heard, go forth, and are choked with cares and riches and pleasures of this life, and bring no fruit to perfection.

Paul writes about this falling away in 1 Timothy 4:1-3:

> 1 Now the Spirit speaketh expressly, that in the latter (end) times some shall depart from the faith, giving heed to seducing spirits, and doctrines of devils;
>
> 2 Speaking lies in hypocrisy, having their conscience seared with a hot iron;
>
> 3 Forbidding to marry, and commanding to abstain from meats, which God hath created to be received with thanksgiving of them which believe and know the truth.

Those who believe and know the truth are the church!

These that fall away are not the church, not the body of Christ. When the scripture says some will depart from the faith, the scripture in context means that some will err from the gospel of grace.

Read the previous verse 1 in context.

Giving heed to seducing spirits and doctrine of demons.

And 1 Timothy 4:3:

> 3 forbidding to marry, and to eat certain foods which God created to be received (by whom?) by those who believe and know the truth (the church).

This is important if we want to understand our relationship with the Lord and to understand that the very nature of God is love.

He loves us and protects us, in these letters as in other scripture he warns us of harmful influences from those outside the body of Christ.

If we are to successfully study these scriptures, we must realize that Jesus never threatened a believer during his earthly ministry, and he does not in the letters to the seven assemblies.

I cannot assume that anyone agrees or disagrees with the following statements regardless of how long they may have been reading the Bible, but I believe that no Pope presided in the early church, especially not Peter.

John the Baptist was not a Christian. He was a prophet under the old covenant, and no Pentecostal denomination existed.

In the New Testament there is no reference to any denomination but only to the body of true believers "the church," where ever they may be.

I have had conversations with friends in person and on social media where they stated that their brand of the Christian faith or denomination is the true faith.

Catholic friends tell me Peter was the first pope, so they have the best faith.

Baptist friends say that John was the founder of the Baptist church, therefore they have the best faith.

Some Pentecostal friends say the true church was born on the day of Pentecost having been baptized with the Holy Spirit and speaking with tongues. True, but are they the best faith?

Such arguments are the pride of mankind being led by the devil to divide the church which also is a poor witness to the world.

Jesus said in Matthew 12:24, "And if Satan cast out Satan, he is divided against himself; how shall then his kingdom stand?"

Jesus spoke those words in response to the religious people of his time who accused him of casting out demons by the power of Satan.

Jesus went on to say that all sin and blasphemy of men would be forgiven except for blaspheming the Holy Spirit, Matthew 12:31-32.

When we call another Christian a wolf in sheep's clothing, we are accusing them of being led of the devil—the very thing Jesus was accused of.

What does this have to do with the love of God and the letters to the seven assemblies?

Everything.

Ephesians 4:4-6

> 4 There is one body, (church) and one (Holy) Spirit, even as ye are called in one hope of your calling;
>
> 5 One Lord, (Jesus) one faith, (grace) one baptism, (in the Holy Spirit)
>
> 6 One God and Father of all, who is above all, and through all, and in you all.

In the letters to the seven assemblies, we see in Revelation 1:20, the KJV translation of the word assemblies translated "churches" plural, that should make the hair on the back of your neck stand up.

There is only one church, not churches.

In context, Jesus is not condemning the church but rather those outside of the church body going to "church" or assembly only, and he does that as an act of love attempting to bring people to his saving grace.

CHAPTER 3

The Throne Room of God

Revelation Chapter Four

A lot of commentators and preachers say this chapter is a picture of the rapture or the catching away of the church.

I don't believe that it is. John was called up to heaven to be a witness to what he sees and hears and he describes the things that he hears and sees in vivid detail.

As he describes the scenes in the throne room of heaven, he repeatedly tells exactly who is present as the events unfold.

> 1 After this I looked, and behold, a door was opened in heaven: and the first voice which I heard was as it were of a trumpet talking with me; (Jesus, Revelation 1:10) which said, Come up hither, and I will shew thee things which must be hereafter.

> 2 And immediately I was in the spirit: and, behold, a throne was set in heaven, and one sat on the throne.

> 3 And he that sat was to look upon like a jasper and sardine stone: and there was a rainbow round about the throne, in sight like unto an emerald.

4 And around the throne were four and twenty seats: and upon the seats I saw four and twenty elders sitting, clothed in white raiment; and they had on their heads crowns of gold.

5 And out of the throne proceeded lightnings and thunderings and voices: and there were seven lamps of fire burning before the throne, which are the seven Spirits (attributes of the Holy Spirit) of God.

6 And before the throne there was a sea of glass like unto crystal; (This is the river of life.) and in the midst of the throne, and round about the throne, were four beasts, full of eyes before and behind.

7 The first beast was like a lion, and the second beast like a calf, (or cherubim Ezekiel 10:14) the third beast had a face as a man, and the fourth beast was like a flying eagle.

8 And the four beasts had each of them six wings about him; and they were full of eyes within: and they rest not day and night, saying: Holy, holy, holy Lord God Almighty, which was, and is, and is to come.

John so far has given us a lot of detail and so far, the only people in the throne room of God is the Lord God, John, and the twenty-four elders along with the four living creatures 30 persons, personality's in all.

The resurrected and raptured saints are not yet in heaven.

9 And when those beasts (living creatures) give glory and honour and thanks to him that sat on the throne, who liveth for ever and ever,

10 The four and twenty elders fall down before him that sat on the throne, and worship him that liveth forever and ever, and cast their crowns before the throne saying,

11 Thou art worthy, O Lord, to receive glory and honour and power: for thou hast created all things, and for thy pleasure they are and were created.

The four created creatures here are special ministers of God's creation, they have six wings, the number of the days of creation and they have the faces of his creation, more about this later.

Revelation Chapter Five

1 And I saw in the right hand of him (God the Father) that sat on the throne a book written within and on the backside, sealed with seven seals.

2 And I saw a strong angel (he just now shows up) proclaiming with a loud voice, Who is worthy to open the book, and loose the seals thereof?

3 And no man in heaven, nor in earth, neither under the earth, was able to open the book, neither look thereon.

4 And I wept much, because no man was found worthy to open and to read the book, neither to look thereon.

5 And one of the elders saith unto me, Weep not: behold, the Lion of the tribe of Juda, the Root of David (Jesus), hath prevailed (overcame death and has the authority) to open the book, and to loose the seven seals thereof

Why would John weep? The scripture says that no one was found worthy but then one of the elders said that the Lion of the tribe of Juda, Jesus had prevailed.

Revelation 19:6 says in part, Alleluia: for the Lord God omnipotent reineth. Jesus doesn't rein in the earth now but only in the lives of some, I believe that is why John wept.

Some say that the seven seals are seven separate individual judgments, but they are not. This book or scroll with the seven seals is a legal document as we will see in the next few verses.

> 5:6 And I beheld, and, lo, in the midst of the throne and the four beasts, (created beings) and in the midst of the elders, stood a Lamb as it had been slain, having seven horns and seven eyes, which are the seven Spirits of God sent forth into all the earth.

> 7 And he came and took the book out of the right hand of him that sat on the throne.

God the Father hands over to Jesus, God the Son, this legal document.

> 8 And when he had taken the book, the four beasts and the four and twenty elders fell down before the Lamb, having every one of them harps, and golden vials full of odours, which are the prayers of the saints.

The saints are still on earth; their prayers are represented in the vials.

> 9 And they (the four living creatures and the elders) sung a new song, saying, Thou art worthy (You have authority) to take the book, and to open the seals thereof: for thou wast slain, (a perfect sacrifice) and hast redeemed us to God (conquering death) by thy (pure) blood out of every kindred, and tongue, and people, and nation;

> 10 And hast made us unto our God kings and priests: and we shall rein on the earth.

> 11 And I beheld, and I heard the voice of many angels round about the throne and the beasts and the elders: and the number of them was ten thousand times ten thousand, and thousands of thousands; (Billions, trillions perhaps, but not all!)

So just now, a multitude of angels show up and we have John, countless angels, a mighty angel, the four beasts or living creatures, the elders and God the Father and God the Son. This is the complete description of the throne room in heaven and there are no resurrected and raptured saints there.

> 5:12 Saying with a loud voice, Worthy is the Lamb that was slain, to receive (authority) power and riches, and wisdom, and strength, and honor, and glory, and blessing.

> 13 And every creature which is in heaven, and on earth, and under the earth, and such as are in the sea, and all that are in them, heard I saying,

From verse 13, on earth and under the earth and such as are in the sea should be a good indication that the resurrection of saints and rapture of the body of believers has not yet happened.

The people on the earth are the yet-to-be raptured saints.

The creatures under the earth are the bodies of the saints that will be caught up to their spirits in the sky according to the apostle Paul in 1 Corinthians 15:51-56 and 2 Thessalonians 4:13-18.

Verse 13 continues with the song of praise.

13 Blessing, and honour, and glory, and power, be unto him that sitteth upon the throne, and unto the Lamb for ever and ever.

14 And the four beasts said, Amen. And the four and twenty elders fell down and worshiped him that liveth for ever and ever.

Beginning with the previous verse 9, the four cherubim and the elders sing a new song, then the multitude of angels join in the praise, then all of God's creation both in heaven and earth sing praise.

I believe that from this point forward, the earth and all of God's creation is progressively being delivered.

These scriptures are what the seven sealed scroll are about, the authority and power given to Christ Jesus as the second Adam to take possession of God's people and deliver his creation.

The words angel and messenger are interchangeable and may refer to the Lord, an angelic spirit, or a human.

A living creature or cherub has wings which represent protection and have a special ministry of the Lord's deliverance of his creation.

Ezekiel describes four living creatures in the first chapter of Ezekiel and these creatures do not speak to him but they precede the Lord who does.

In Chapter 10, he describes the same four living creatures as cherubim where once again they do not speak until asked, but appear with the glory of the Lord.

These four look like the ones in the throne room but only have four wings, whereas the ones in heaven minister in heaven, these four minister on earth and are described as having wheels and hubs or rims.

Elijah was taken into heaven in 2 Kings 2:11: Behold, there appeared a chariot of fire, and horses of fire ...

The description of horses and chariots is critical in understanding Revelation chapters six and seven.

Let's go to Zechariah 1:8-11

> 8 I saw by night, (in a dream) and behold a man riding upon a red horse, and he stood among the myrtle trees that were in the bottom; and behind him were there red horses, speckled, and white.

Only three colors in this vision but four sets of horses.

> 9 Then said I, O my lord, what are these? And the angel (messenger) that talked with me said unto me, I will shew thee what these be.

> 10 And the man that stood among the myrtle trees answered and said, These are they whom the LORD hath sent to walk to and fro through the earth.

> 11 And they answered the angel of the LORD that stood among the myrtle trees, and said, We have walked to and fro through the earth, and, behold, all the earth sitteth still, and is at rest.

I believe the angel of the Lord is Jesus, v. 9 ... O my lord, what are these? Then in v. 10 ... These are they whom the LORD hath sent ... and v. 11 And they answered the angel of the LORD that stood among the myrtle trees, ...

The Lord sent the horsemen and the horsemen report to the angel of the lord with a small l, but I believe that pastor Robert Morris is correct that the angel of the Lord is always Jesus.

Now from Zechariah 6:1-5

> 1 And I turned, and lifted up my eyes, and looked, and, behold, there came four chariots out from between two mountains; and the mountains were mountains of brass.
>
> 2 In the first chariot were red horses; and in the second chariot black horses;
>
> 3 And in the third chariot white horses; and in the fourth chariot grisled (grayish) and bay horses.
>
> 4 Then I answered and said unto the angel that talked with me, What are these, my lord?
>
> 5 And the angel answered and said unto me, These are the four spirits (or winds) of the heavens, which go forth from standing before the Lord of all the earth.

From the context, the four chariots that go out from between two mountains of bronze and the four spirits of heaven going out from standing in the presence of the Lord indicates the mountains of brass are God the Father and God the Son in righteous judgment.

See Daniel 2:39, a kingdom of brass, and the mountain of God in Exodus 18:5.

Numbers 21:9 portrays Jesus as a brass serpent put on a pole. This symbolism is a type and shadow of Christ crucified on a tree receiving the judgment of God.

Revelation 17:9: And here is the mind which has wisdom. The seven heads are seven mountains, ... v.10 and there are seven kings:

So the interpretation of mountain in many scriptures is king or kingdom, power or the seat of power.

Beginning in Revelation 6:9, the prophesy does not follow in chronological order by chapter and verse. I will put these events in chronological order.

CHAPTER 4

Jesus opens the seals

John continues to witness the events that he sees and hears in heaven, Jesus takes the scroll from his Father God and only he has the right and authority to open the seals.

Some folks preach and teach that the seven seals on the scroll are seven independent judgments that are released when Jesus opens the seals.

In my opinion they are not, this idea of the seals representing individual judgments is one more of the almost universally accepted but incorrect notions among the evangelical church. Another one is that the rider on the white horse is the antichrist, I believe that the following scriptures will clarify any discrepancy.

Revelation Chapter Six

> 1 And I saw when the Lamb opened one of the seven seals, and I heard, as it were the noise of thunder, one of the four beasts saying, Come and see.
>
> 2 And I saw, and behold a white horse: and he that sat on him had a bow; and a crown was given unto him, (the angel) and he went forth conquering and to conquer.

This is not the man antichrist; this is an angel.

> 3 When he (Jesus), had opened the second seal, I heard the second beast say, Come and see.
>
> 4 And there went out another horse, that was red: and power was given to him that sat thereon to take peace from the earth and that they should kill one another: and there was given unto him a great sword.

If the rider on the white horse is the man antichrist, who is this?

> 5 And when he had opened the third seal, I heard the third beast say, Come and see. And I beheld and lo a black horse; And he that sat on him (the angel) had a pair of balances in his hand.
>
> 6 And I heard a voice in the midst of the four beast say, A measure of wheat for a penny, (a day's wages) and three measures of barley for a penny; see thou hurt not the oil and the wine. Is this rider the head of The World Trade Organization?
>
> 7 And when he had opened the fourth seal, I heard the voice from the fourth beast say, Come and see.
>
> 8 And I looked and behold, a pale horse: (or green, really—the color or lack of color of a dead person): and his name that sat on him was Death (a proper name), and Hell followed with him. And power was given unto (the four of) them over the fourth part of the (geography of) earth to kill with sword, and with hunger, and with death, (all kinds of plague) and with the beast of the earth.

The beasts of the earth aren't diseases—they are animals or predators. This is one particular judgment.

Again, these are not seal judgments. The angels or horsemen are spiritual beings that operate in the realm of the spirit to set up and carry out the judgments when God calls for the trumpets to blow during the great tribulation in the second half of the seven years.

As the Lord opens the first four seals the six-winged cherubs call fourth the horsemen who will go throughout the earth to do the Lord's will.

In verse eight, a fourth part of the earth is exactly that: one quarter of the geography of the earth, not the population as some teach.

In his description of events from the beginning, John is precise. He describes the judgments, the people effected, and the numbers of people as the events unfold in his revelation.

World War I was not fought on the face of the entire world, and neither was World War II. No battlefield has ever encompassed the entire globe.

The opening of the fifth and sixth seals occur in chronological order but they are prophetic events near the end of the tribulation. We will address them in detail after we complete the study of the first four seals which are explained in the following chapter.

Revelation Chapter Seven

> 1 And after these things I saw four angels standing on the four corners of the earth, holding the four winds (spirits) of the earth, that the wind (cherubim) should not blow on the earth, nor on any tree. (Jeremiah 49:36)

Daniel 7:2 behold, the four winds (cherubim, angels or spirits) of heaven strove upon the great sea (of nations).

> 2 And I saw another angel ascending from the east, having the seal of the living God: and he cried out with a loud voice to the four angels to whom it was given to hurt the earth and the sea,

Four angels are sent to hold back the four winds that they shouldn't blow on the earth or on any tree, and another angel calls out to the four angels who were given power to hurt the earth and sea.

> 3 Saying, hurt not the earth, nor the sea, nor the trees, till we have sealed the servants of our God in their foreheads.

And what is the first judgment recorded in the Revelation?

Revelation 8:7: the first trumpet, a third of the trees are burnt up, and all the green grass. v. 8 the second trumpet, a third of the sea became blood. These events take place late in the second half of the tribulation.

These four winds are the four horsemen of the first four seals in chapter 6.

The four horsemen have been given authority to affect the global geopolitical makeup of the nations, primarily the angel on the white horse as he was given a crown.

And together they take peace from the earth and cause men to kill one another. The angel on the red horse is not killing people. He sets up the events to bring war so that men kill one another.

The horsemen bring famine and disease. The rider on the black horse is followed by Death and Hell, the angel on the pale green horse.

But in verses 2-3, the four angels are told to hold up, so a pre-tribulation resurrection and rapture hasn't happened yet. If the rapture had happened in chapter four, the horsemen would be free to begin their assignment.

If you believe that the rapture took place in chapter 4, you could assume that the seals are individual judgments.

Continuing Chapter Seven

> 4 And I heard the number of them which were sealed: and there were sealed an hundred and forty and four thousand of all the tribes of the children of Israel.

These people are not the church, they are not Christians, and they are not the new Israel. Some people believe that God has replaced Israel with the church, but from the following text the information is clear that they are the descendants of Israel, or Jacob.

> 5 Of the tribe of Juda were sealed twelve thousand. Of the tribe of Ruben were sealed twelve thousand. Of the tribe of Gad were sealed twelve thousand.

> 6 Of the tribe of Aser were sealed twelve thousand. Of the tribe of Nephthalim were sealed twelve thousand. Of the tribe of Manasses were sealed twelve thousand.

> 7 Of the tribe of Simeon were sealed twelve thousand. Of the tribe of Levi were sealed twelve thousand. Of the tribe of Issachar were sealed twelve thousand.

> 8 Of the tribe of Zabulon were sealed twelve thousand. Of the tribe of Joseph were sealed twelve thousand. Of the tribe of Benjamin were sealed twelve thousand.

The 144,000 must be sealed prior to, or at the very instant of, the rapture to protect them and seal them with the Holy Spirit for ministry. They are not Christians, otherwise they would be caught up, raptured with the Christian saints weather Jew or gentile.

The Rapture

Chapter 7:9 through 17 is the pre-tribulation resurrection and rapture of the saints.

> 9 After this (immediately) I beheld, and lo, a great multitude which no man could number, of all nations, and kindreds, and peoples, and tongues, stood before the throne, and before the Lamb, (already) clothed with white robes and palms in their hands;

The resurrected and raptured saints are now standing in front of the throne of God.

Who's in the throne room of God now? Read from the previous v. 9 through 17.

> 10 And cried with a loud voice, saying, Salvation (deliverance, preservation, safety) to our God, which sitteth on the throne, and to the Lamb.

> 11 And all (all) the angels stood round about the throne, and about the elders and the four beasts, and fell before the throne on their faces, and worshiped God,

And now All the angels are in the throne room of God!

> 12 Saying, Amen: Blessing, and glory, and wisdom, and thanksgiving, and honour, and power, and might, be unto our God for ever and ever. Amen.

> 13 And one of the elders answered saying unto me, What are these which are (already) arrayed in white

robes? and whence came they? (where did they come from?)

14 And I said unto him, Sir, thou knowest. And he said to me, these are they which came out of great tribulation, and have washed their robes and made them white in the blood of the Lamb.

Notice this is a great multitude, countless in fact, already dressed in white clothes washed in the blood of Christ. They were snatched out of the earth and caught up to heaven prior to the start of tribulation.

If you go into the tribulation, you may likely end up dead unless you are a faithful Jew in Israel or one of the 144,000, going into the tribulation.

Luke 17:24-37

24 For as the lightning, that lighteneth out of the one part under heaven, shineth unto the other part under heaven; so shall also the Son of man be in his day.

26 And as it was in the day of Noe ...

28 Likewise also as it was in the days of Lot ...

32 Remember Lot's wife.

33 whosoever shall seek to save his life will lose it ...

34 the one shall be taken, and the other shall be left. (raptured or left behind)

Now back to Revelation 7

Rapture

> 7:15 Therefore are they before (in front of) the throne of God, (in heaven) and serve him night and day in his temple: (dwelling place) and he that sitteth on the throne shall dwell among them.

> 16 They hunger no more, neither thirst any more; neither shall the sun light on them, nor any heat.

Because they will not be on earth during the tribulation!

> 17 For the Lamb which is in the midst (middle) of the throne shall feed them, and shall lead them unto living fountains of waters: (The river of life.) And God will wipe away all tears from their eyes.

The seventh seal is next in chapter 8:1, but why is all of chapter 7 written between the opening of the sixth seal in chapter 6 and the seventh seal in chapter 8:1?

Let's go back now to open the fifth and sixth seals in Revelation Chapter 6.

> 9 And when he had opened the fifth seal,

The fifth seal is not a seal judgment. These people die by rejecting the antichrist and the mark of the beast.

> v. 9 continues, I saw under the alter the souls of them that were slain for the word of God (The gospel of Jesus), and for the testimony (confession of faith) which they held:

> 10 And they cried with a loud voice, saying How long O Lord, holy and true, dost thou not judge and avenge our (martyred) blood on them that dwell on the earth?

> 11 And white robes were given unto every one of them; and it was said unto them, that they should rest yet for a little season, until their fellow servants also and their brethren, that should be killed as they were, should be fulfilled.

These martyrs are told to wait UNTIL THE NUMBER OF THEIR FELLOW SERVANTS AND BROTHERS WHO WERE TO BE KILLED as they were was completed and then the judgment of Armageddon will come to the antichrist and the ungodly.

Let's examine the fifth seal in Ch. 6:9-11 'Under the alter, the souls' of those slain, they were then given white robes and waiting for the rest of those who were going to die.

These are the people who come to Christ after the rapture and are killed in the second half of the tribulation's seven-year time period.

Revelation 13:5-7

> 5 And there was given unto him (antichrist) a mouth speaking great things and blasphemies; and power was given unto him to continue forty and two months (three-and-a-half years).

> 6 And he opened his mouth in blasphemy against God, to blaspheme his name, and his tabernacle, (dwelling) and them that dwell in heaven.

> 7 And it was given unto him to make war with the saints, and to overcome them: and power was given him over all kindreds, and tongues, and nations.

Compare these martyred tribulation saints to the pre-tribulation rapture saints in Ch. 7:9-10. A great multitude that no one could count standing before the throne, not under the throne and not disembodied souls, and already wearing white robes.

The sixth seal, Revelation Chapter Six

> 12 And I beheld when he had opened the sixth seal,

This is not a separate seal judgment; this is the judgment of the wicked at Armageddon. v. 12 continues,

> and lo, there was a great earthquake; and the sun turned black as sackcloth of hair, the moon became as blood;

> 13 And the stars of heaven fell unto the earth, even as a fig tree casteth her untimely figs, when she is shaken of a mighty wind.

> 14 And the heaven departed as a scroll when it is rolled together; and every mountain and island was removed out of their places.

> 15 And the kings of the earth, and the great men, and the chief captains, and the rich men, and the mighty men, and every bond man, and every free man, hid in the dens and in the rocks of the mountains;

> 16 And said to the mountains and the rocks, Fall on us (cover us) and hide us from the face of him that sitteth on the throne, and from the wrath of the Lamb:

> 17 For the great day of his wrath is come; and who shall be able to stand?

Once again this is a future event in fact this is the last day of the tribulation period, compare this scripture with the last-day scriptures next.

Revelation 16:16-20

16 And he gathered them together into a place that in the Hebrew tongue is called Armageddon.

17 And the seventh angel poured out his vial into the air; and there came a great voice out of the temple of heaven, from the throne, saying, It is done.

18 And there were voices, and thunders, and lightnings; and there was a great earthquake, such as was not since men were upon the earth, so mighty earthquake, and so great.

(a great earthquake, as never before)

19 And the great city was divided into three parts, and the cities of the nations fell:

20 And every island fled away, and the mountains were not found.

Revelation Chapter Eight

Jesus opens the Seventh Seal

> 1 When he had opened the seventh seal, there was silence in heaven for about the space of half an hour.

If the seven seals are seven individual or separate judgments where is the judgment here?

As I recall In his book *The Late Great Planet Earth*, Hal Lindsay I believe correctly addresses the first half of the tribulation as the half an hour of silence in heaven.

In this case a half an hour is not thirty minutes, it's half of a specific time. Luke 22:53: When I was daily with you in the temple, you stretched forth no hands against me: but this is your hour, (time) and the power of darkness.

Compare that with John 12:27 Now is my heart troubled; and what shall I say? Father, save me from this hour: (time) but for this cause came I to this hour. (time)

The same word used for time is translated hour as in the following verses,

John 5:25 and 16:32 Behold, the hour cometh, yea is now come ...

Revelation 3:10: To the assembly in Philadelphia, (the church in brotherly love.) I also will keep thee from the hour of temptation (time of tribulation), which shall come upon all the world, to try them that dwell upon the earth.

Not that these people in Philadelphia would live to see the tribulation but they are an example of the true and blessed church.

This half an hour of Revelation 8:1 literally represents the first half of the tribulation.

Daniel 8:19: And he said, Behold, I will make thee know what shall be in the last end of the indignation: for at the time appointed the end shall be.

Daniel 9:27: And he (antichrist) shall confirm the covenant with many for one week: (seven) And in the midst of the week (seven years) he shall cause the sacrifice and the oblation to cease, ...

We know from this scripture that there will also be a temple in Jerusalem during the tribulation.

From Daniel 12:7, we know the middle of the seven is for a time, times and half a time.

And Revelation Ch. 12:6, 1,260 days, Ch. 13:5, forty and two months or three-and-a-half years.

So what does the book of Revelation say about the first half of the tribulation?

Really nothing, but we can assume that the 144,000 from the twelve tribes of Israel will preach the coming of Messiah.

The church is gone, caught up, raptured and Jesus turns his affection back to Israel, the 144,000 will preach the same gospel message that Jesus and his disciples did first to the Jews and then to the Gentiles.

Matthew 10:5-8

> 5 These twelve Jesus sent forth, and commanded them, saying, Go not into the way of the Gentiles, and into any city of the Samaritans enter ye not:
>
> 6 But go rather, to the lost sheep of the house of Israel.
>
> 7 And as ye go, preach, saying, The kingdom of heaven is at hand.
>
> 8 Heal the sick, cleanse the lepers, raise the dead, cast out devils: freely ye have received, freely give.

But now he sends twelve times twelve thousand. Matthew 24:14: And this gospel of the kingdom shall be preached in all the world for a witness unto all nations; and then the end shall come.

Everything recorded in the book of Revelation concerning the details of the tribulation begins at mid-tribulation.

The book of Revelation has 8 of 22 chapters dedicated wholly or at least in part to the events that occur at the three-and-a-half-year mid-tribulation period, so naturally many of the events will overlap.

These eight chapters are given specific timelines or are tied to events that are tied to the timelines; this is made clear from the text.

The prophesy does not follow the order of chapter and verse but once we see the scriptures in chronological order the prophecy becomes clear.

CHAPTER 5:

Mid-tribulation

Revelation 14:1-13 the mid-tribulation rapture

> 1 And I looked, and, lo, (in heaven) a Lamb, stood on the (heavenly) mount Sion, and with him an hundred forty and four thousand, having (the seal of) his Father's name written in their foreheads.
>
> 2 And I heard a voice from heaven, as the voice of many waters and as the voice of a great thunder: and I heard the voice of harpers harping with their harps:
>
> 3 And they (the 144,000) sung as it were a new song before (in the presence of) the throne, and before (in the presence of) the four beasts, and the elders: (in heaven)
>
> 4 And no man could learn that song but the hundred and forty and four thousand, which were redeemed (purchased) from the earth.

God's people are not appointed to his wrath and these saints were sealed at the time of the rapture, and the tribulation had not yet started, this is the mid-tribulation rapture of the 144,000 from the twelve tribes of Israel.

Just like the scene from the throne room in heaven in Revelation chapters 5:8-10, 7:9 and 15:2-3 they are literally in front of the throne and they sing a new song.

Back to Chapter 14:4

These are they which were not defiled with women; for they are virgins. These are they which follow the Lamb whithersoever he goeth. These were redeemed from among men, being first fruits (of a new harvest) unto God and to the Lamb.

> 5 And in their mouth was found no guile: for they are without fault before the throne of God.

Jesus had no perfect apostles, and these aren't perfect except through Christ as we are.

I believe it's clear from the context that these are apostles of Christ, they are the first fruit of the new harvest of the descendants of Israel (Jacob).

> 6 And I saw another angel fly in the midst of heaven, (the sky) having the everlasting gospel to preach unto them that dwell on the earth, and to every nation, and kindred, and tongue, and people,

Because the 144,000 have been taken up and Satan is now cast down to earth God sends an angel to literally warn the people on the earth, in verse 7.

Satan is cast down to earth at mid-tribulation, Revelation 12:13 and 14:

> 13 And when the dragon saw that he was cast unto the earth, he persecuted the woman (Israel) which brought forth the man child (Jesus).

> 14 And to the woman were given two wings of a great eagle, so that she might fly to the wilderness, into her place, were she is nourished for a time, and times, and half a time (3.5 years), from the face of the serpent (Satan).

Back to Revelation Fourteen

> 7 Saying with a loud voice, Fear God, and give glory to him; for the hour of his judgment is come:

At the end of these mid-tribulation chapters will come the trumpet judgments, 7 continues,

> Worship him that made heaven, and earth, and the sea, and the fountains of waters.

> 8 And there followed another angel, saying, Babylon is fallen, is fallen that great city, because she made all nations drink of the wine of the wrath of her fornication.

This begins at mid-tribulation; this is not a city or a religion, it is the world's economic system.

> 9 And the third angel followed them, saying with a loud voice, If any man worship the beast and his image, and receive his mark in his forehead or in his hand,

The mark of the beast comes at mid-tribulation.

> 10 The same shall drink of the wine of the wrath of God, which is poured out without mixture into the cup of his indignation; and he shall be tormented with fire and brimstone in the presence of the holy angels, and in the presence of the Lamb:

> 11 And the smoke of their torment ascendeth up forever and forever: and they have no rest day or night, (those) who worship the beast and his image, and whosoever receiveth the mark of his name.
>
> 12 Here is the patience of the (tribulation) saints: here are they that keep the commandments of God, and the faith of Jesus.
>
> 13 And I heard a voice from heaven saying unto me, Write, Blessed are the dead which die in the Lord from henceforth: (they are better off dead) Yea, saith the Spirit, that they may rest from their labours; and their works (of faith) do follow them.

Referencing the timeline of events during the tribulation, see what Jesus had to say in Matthew 24:15-16

> 15 When ye therefore shall see the abomination of desolation, spoken of by Daniel the prophet, stand in the holy place (whoso readeth, let him understand).
>
> 16 Then let them which are in Judea (Israel) flee into the mountains:

We see in the following Revelation chapter 11 that the abomination spoken of by Daniel lasts forty- two months or three-and-a-half years, this event must occur during the second half of the tribulation.

The gentile saints are not protected from the antichrist but the faithful Jews of Israel are as we will soon see in Revelation chapter 12.

Revelation Chapter 11:1-6 (Mid-tribulation)

> 1 And there was given unto me a reed like unto a rod: and the angel stood saying, Rise, and measure the temple of God, and the alter, and them that worship therein.

There will be the temple built in Jerusalem during the first half of the tribulation if not sooner.

> 2 But the court which is without the temple leave out, and measure it not; for it given unto the Gentiles: and the holy city shall they tread under foot forty and two months. (timeline)

> 3 And I will give power unto my two witnesses, and they shall prophesy a thousand two hundred and three score days, clothed in sackcloth.

Timeline; 3.5 years, these two take over where the 144,000 left off.

> 4 These are the two olive trees, and the two candlesticks standing before the God of the earth.

Prophets not assemblies in this case, the church is gone.

> 5 And if any man will hurt them, fire proceedeth out of their mouth, and devoureth their enemies: and if any man will hurt them, he must in this manner be killed.

> 6 These have power to shut heaven that it rain not in the days of their prophesy: and have power over waters to turn them to blood, and smite the earth with all plagues, as often as they will.

Their ability to work miracles during the second half of tribulation is tied to the seal judgments which start immediately following these mid-tribulation events.

Revelation Chapter 12 (Mid-tribulation)

Chapters 12 and 13 run together, starting with some historical record written in symbolism. Symbolism is found throughout Bible prophecy and is not without meaning.

The woman, the nation of Israel gave birth to the Messiah Jesus and Satan tried to have him killed.

The nation of Israel is now back in their own land and is in the great tribulation, Satan and a third of the angels are cast down to earth.

Satan is angry with Israel and sets out to destroy her, but God protects her so he goes after the gentile believers or non-Israelis which may include the so-called lost tribes of Israel who have come to faith in Jesus by the preaching of the 144,000 evangelists during the first half of the tribulation.

> 12:1 And there appeared a great wonder in heaven; a woman (Israel) clothed with the sun, and the moon under her feet, and upon her head a crown of twelve stars:

Jesus is the sun that the woman Israel is clothed with, Malachi 4:2 the Sun of righteousness, the greater light of God's creation, and the moon under her feet is the lesser light of his creation, the reflection of his glory through the saints of God. And the crown of stars are the twelve tribes of Israel.

> 2 And she being with child (Messiah, Jesus) cried, travailing in birth, and pained to be delivered.

> 3 And there appeared another wonder in heaven; and behold, a great red dragon (Satan), having seven heads

> and ten horns, and seven crowns upon his heads. (Daniel 7:8)

> 4 And his tail drew the third part of the stars (angels) of heaven, and did cast them to the earth:

Daniel 8:10 And it waxed great, even to the host of heaven; and it cast down some of the host and of the stars (angels) to the ground and stamped upon them.

v. 4 continues,

> and the dragon stood before the woman which was ready to be delivered, for to devour her child as soon as it was born. (King Herod, Matthew 2:13-18)

> 5 And she brought forth a man child, (Jesus, Matthew 1:25) who was to rule the nations with a rod of iron: and her child was (harpazo, snatched) caught up unto God, and to his throne.

> Mark 16:19: So then after the Lord had spoken unto them, he was received up into heaven, and sat on the right hand of God.

Revelation Chapter Twelve continues

> 6 And the woman (Israel) fled into the wilderness, where she hath a place prepared of God, that they should feed her there a thousand two hundred and three score days (Timeline, 3 .5 years).

Once again from Matthew 24:16 and 21: then let them which are in Judea (Israel) flee to the mountains: v. 21 For then shall be great tribulation, such as was not since the beginning of the world to this time, no, nor ever shall be,—Great tribulation as never before and never again will be.

7 And there was war in heaven: Michael and his angels fought against the dragon; and the dragon fought and his angels (during the tribulation),

8 And (Satan) prevailed not; neither was their place found any more in heaven.

9 And the great dragon was cast out, (of heaven) that old serpent, called the Devil, and Satan, which deceiveth the whole world: he was cast out into the earth, and his angels were cast out with him (at mid-tribulation).

10 And I heard a loud voice saying in heaven, Now is come salvation, and strength, and the kingdom of our God, and the power of his Christ: for the accuser of our brethren is cast down, which accused them before our God day and night. (Job 1:6)

11 And they (the saints in heaven) overcame him by the (saving) blood of the Lamb, and by the word of their testimony; they loved not their lives unto the death (the martyred saints),

12 Therefor rejoice, ye heavens, and ye (saints) that dwell in them. Woe to the inhabitants of the earth and of the sea! for the devil is (just now) come down unto you, having great wrath, because he knoweth that he hath but a short time (3.5 years),

Luke 10:18 And he (Jesus) said unto them, (his disciples) I beheld Satan as lightning fall from heaven.

13 When the dragon saw he was cast unto the earth, (Isaiah 14:12) he persecuted the woman (Israel) which brought forth the man child. (Jesus)

> 14 And to the woman were given two wings of a great eagle,

Some people teach that the wings of an eagle represents the USA using jet airplanes to evacuate the Jews.

This is not the USA. This is God working like he has done in the past. Exodus 19:4 Ye have seen what I did unto the Egyptians, and how I bare you on eagles wings and brought you unto myself.

14 (continued) that she might fly into the wilderness, into her place, where she is nourished (taken care of) for a time and times and half a time, (3.5 years) from the face of the serpent.

This protection is for the faithful of Israel not the rest of the people of the world, Ezekiel 38-39, which we will cover later in this book.

> 15 And the serpent cast out of his mouth water (an army, Revelation 17:1) as a flood, after the woman, that he might cause her to be carried away with the flood.

Isaiah 59:19 When the enemy shall come in like a flood, the Spirit of the Lord shall lift up a standard against him.

> 16 And the earth helped the woman, and the earth opened her mouth, (Numbers 16:30-35) and swallowed up the flood (army) which the dragon cast (spake) out of his mouth.

> 17 And the dragon was wroth with the woman, (because he failed) and went to make war with the remnant of her seed, which keep the commandments of God, and have the testimony of Jesus Christ.

The remnant of her seed are the non-Israeli believers who come to faith during the tribulation.

Revelation Chapter 13 (Mid-tribulation)

Chapter 12 is continued here in chapter 13.

The antichrist is now fully possessed by Satan and he goes out to kill the Jews but God delivers them out of his hand, so he pursues the believers of the nations and is successful.

He demands people receive the mark of his name in order to buy or sell and a false prophet comes to power to enforce the worship of the antichrist under penalty of death.

> 1 And I stood upon the sand of the sea, (the edge of the nations, Revelation 17:1) and saw a beast rise up out of the sea (nations) having seven heads and ten horns, and upon his horns ten crowns, and upon his heads the name of blasphemy. (Daniel 7:8 & 19-25)

> 2 And the beast which I saw was like unto a leopard, (Greece, Alexander the Great) and his feet were as the feet of a bear, (Medo-Persia) and his mouth as the mouth of a lion: (Babylon) and the dragon gave him (antichrist) his power, and his seat, and great authority.

> 3 And I saw one of his heads (antichrist) as it were wounded to death; and his deadly wound was healed:

This leader or head is the antichrist as found in Zechariah 11:17 Woe to the idol shepherd (leader) that leaveth the flock! The sword shall be upon his arm, and upon his right eye: his arm shall be clean dried up, and his right eye shall be utterly darkened.

> 13:3 and all the world wondered after the beast.

> 4 And they worshiped the dragon (Satan) which gave power unto the beast (Antichrist): and they worshiped the beast saying, who is like unto the beast? who is able to make war with him?

> 5 And there was given unto him a mouth speaking great things and blasphemies; and power was given unto him to continue forty and two months. (3.5 years, our timeline)
>
> 6 And he opened his mouth to blaspheme against God, to blaspheme his name, and his tabernacle, and them that dwell in heaven.
>
> 7 And it was given unto him to make war with the (tribulation) saints, and to overcome them: and power was given him over all kindreds, and tongues, and nations;

Because they had previously rejected the gospel of Jesus they missed the rapture.

> 8 And all that dwell upon the earth shall worship him, whose names have not been written in the book of life of the Lamb slain from the foundation of the world.
>
> 9 If any man have an ear, let him hear.
>
> 10 He that leadeth into captivity, shall go into captivity: he that killeth with the sword, must be killed with the sword. Here is the patience and the faith of the saints.

To survive during the tribulation, a person will have to absolutely trust and rely on Jesus for provision and protection. This is true even now, but then the rule of law is out of the hands of mankind and taking up your AK or AR 15 will not be the answer to your survival.

> 11 And I beheld another beast (the false prophet) coming up out of the earth; (Israel) (Revelation 10:2)

> and he had two horns like a lamb, but he spake as a dragon.

> 12 He exerciseth all the power of the first beast before him, and causeseth the earth and those which dwell therein to worship the first beast, whose deadly wound was healed.

Why would I speculate the beast coming up out of the earth is the land of Israel?

The beast and the false prophet aren't setting up shop in Vatican City but at the temple in Jerusalem. The church is gone, and Jesus isn't coming again for the church, he's coming as the son of David the conquering King of Israel.

Again, in Matthew 24:15 When ye therefore shall see the abomination of desolation, spoken of by Daniel the prophet …

There will be three-and-a-half years from mid-tribulation to Armageddon, this is the great tribulation.

> 13:13 And he doeth great wonders, so that he maketh fire come down from heaven on the earth in the sight of men.

> 14 And he deceiveth them that dwell on the earth by the means of those miracles which he had power to do in the sight of the beast; saying to them that dwell on the earth, that they should make an image to the beast, which had the wound by a sword and did live.

> 15 And he had power to give life unto the image of the beast, that the image of the beast should both speak, and cause that as many as would not worship the image of the beast should be killed. (Matthew 24:15-16 and Revelation 6:9)

16 And he causeth all, both small and great, rich and poor, free and bond, to receive a mark in their right hand, or in their foreheads:

17 And that no man might buy or sale save he that had the mark, or the name of the beast, or the number of his name.

18 Here is wisdom. Let him that hath understanding, (by the Holy Spirit) count the number of the beast: for it is the number of a man; and his number is six hundred three score and six (666).

I doubt that this man will be revealed by God until after the rapture but probably during the first three and half years, I don't believe that our Father will leave the world without a way of escape.

Revelation Chapter 17 (Mid-tribulation)

All of chapters 17 and 18 have a common theme and share the same subject, God's judgment of the world's economic system carried out by Satan, the antichrist and the ten rulers. At some point the antichrist will overthrow three of the ten leaders.

And the antichrist will establish his own economy with the mark of the beast.

The world's economy will be wrecked bringing on the worst depression of all time, this new world order is tied to six past world powers making this one the seventh.

Satan has been a part of them all thus he is the eighth and is a part of the seven.

There is a lot of symbolism portrayed, Babylon the prostitute is the present economy the beast is the antichrist the dragon is Satan and the beast with two horns is the false prophet.

The former world powers are depicted as animals pictured in the prophesy of Daniel 7:4-8.

> 17:1 And there came one of the seven angels which had the seven vials, and talked with me, saying unto me, Come hither; I will shew unto thee the judgment of the great whore (Revelation 14:8-10) that sitteth on many waters. (nations, peoples and languages)
>
> 2 With whom the kings of the earth have committed fornication, and the inhabitants of the earth have been made drunk with the wine of her fornication. (spiritual adultery)
>
> 3 So he (the angel) carried me away in the spirit into the wilderness: and I saw a woman sit upon a scarlet coloured beast, full of names of blasphemy, having seven heads and ten horns.

This woman is the world's economic system sitting symbolically on the antichrist and the nations of this satanic world power.

Daniel 7:24-25

> 24 And the ten horns out of this kingdom are ten kings that shall arise: and another shall arise after them (antichrist); and he shall be diverse from the first, (kings) and he shall subdue three kings.

So ten kings are ten horns plus one is eleven, minus three equals eight kings of this kingdom.

> 25 And he shall speak great words against the most High, and shall wear out the saints of the most High, and think to change times and the laws: and they (the tribulation saints) shall be given into his hand until a

time and times and the dividing of time. (three-and-a-half years)

Revelation Chapter Seventeen continues

4 And the woman was arrayed in purple and scarlet colour, (royalty) and decked with gold, and precious stones and pearls (wealth), having a golden cup in her hand full of abominations and filthiness of her fornication: (spiritual adultery)

5 And upon her forehead was a name written, MYSTERY, BABYLON THE GREAT, THE MOTHER OF HARLOTS AND ABOMINATIONS OF THE EARTH.

6 And I saw the woman drunken with the blood of the saints, and with the blood of the martyrs of Jesus: and when I saw her, I wondered with great admiration.

7 And the angel said unto me, wherefore didst thou marvel? I will tell thee the mystery of the woman, and the beast that carrieth her, which hath seven heads and ten horns.

8 The beast that thou sawest was, and is not; and shall ascend out of the bottomless pit, and go into perdition: and they that dwell on the earth shall wonder, whose names were not written in the book of life from the foundation of the world, when they behold the beast, that was, and is not, and yet is.

This scarlet beast or dragon is Satan, and he is joined with antichrist and the leaders of this kingdom or world influencing power.

> 9 And here is the mind which hath wisdom. The seven heads are seven mountains, (nations powers kingdoms) on which the woman sits.

The seven heads are the seven symbolic mountains of power, they are not the seven hills of Rome as some teach. Zechariah 4:7 Isaiah 14:13 and 24:21.

> 10 And there are seven kings: (or kingdoms) five are fallen (Egypt, Assyria, Babylon, Persia and Greece under Alexander the Great), and one is, (Rome, in John's time) and the other is not yet come; and when he cometh, he must continue a short space (three-and-a half years, the seventh kingdom).

The LITTLE HORN of Daniel 7:8 is the beast, the man #666 of the tribulation period.

> 11 And the beast that was, and is not, (Satan) even he is the eighth, and is of the seven, (powers nations kingdoms) and goeth into perdition.

Eternal destruction, in the lake of fire.

Revelation 20:1-3

> 1 And I saw an angel come down from heaven, having the key to the bottomless pit and a great chain in his hand …

> 2 And he laid hold on the dragon, that old serpent (the beast that was), who is the Devil and Satan, and bound him for a thousand years,

> 3 And cast him into the bottomless pit (hell), and shut him up (the beast who now is not), and set a seal upon him, that he should deceive the nations no more, till

> the thousand years should be fulfilled: and after that he must be loosed a little season.

The beast 'who will come' up from the bottomless pit and is going to his destruction will be cast into the lake of fire in the end.

Revelation Chapter 17 continues

> 12 And the ten horns which thou sawest are ten kings, which have received no kingdom as yet; but receive power as kings one hour with the beast.

Seven years, one hour, a specific period of time.

Daniel 7:24 and 25, the antichrist will overthrow three of the kings. 25 the antichrist will rule for a time and times and half a time.

> 13 These (10 kings) have one mind, and shall give their power and strength unto the beast.

> 14 These shall make war with the Lamb, and the Lamb shall overcome them: (at Armageddon) for he is Lord of lords, and King of kings: and they that are with him are called, and chosen, and faithful.

The Church and the saints of all time

> 15 And he sayeth unto me, The waters which thou sawest, were the whore sitteth, are peoples, multitudes, nations and tongues.

Here we have the symbol of waters defined as peoples, multitudes, nations and languages, make a note of this.

> 16 And the ten horns which thou sawest upon the beast, these shall hate the whore (the present economy), and they shall make her desolate and naked, and shall eat her flesh, and burn her with fire.

The woman Babylon the Great, the prostitute is not a religious system she is the world's economic system which some people have made into an idol and do idolize.

Satan, the beast, and the rulers want all the power and control so they destroy her and set up the mark of the beast and demand that people worship the beast.

> 17:17 For God hath put it in their (10 kings) hearts to fulfil his will, and to agree, and give their kingdom to the beast, until the words of God shall be fulfilled.

> 18 And the woman which thou sawest is that great city, which reineth over the kings of the earth.

This is why they hate her, because she is the global economy and rules over the nations. Babylon is not New York or Hong Kong, if the beast "antichrist" is going to require everyone to receive his mark in order to buy or sell he must replace the present global economic system.

The new economy doesn't need to be accepted by all nations to impact the economies of all nations.

God doesn't like this system either, because under her, we are slaves to debt, compound interest and a thirty-year-mortgage.

Revelation Chapter Eighteen (mid-tribulation)

(Basically chapter 17 continued)

> 1 And after these things I saw another angel come down from heaven, having great power; and the earth was lightened with his glory.

> 2 And he cried mightily with a strong voice, saying, Babylon the great is fallen, is fallen, and is become the habitation of devils, and the hold of every foul spirit, and a cage of every unclean and hateful bird.

> 3 For all nations have drunk of the wine of the wrath of her fornication, and the kings of the earth have committed (spiritual) fornication with her, and the merchants of the earth are waxed (grown) rich through the abundance of her delicacies.

> 4 And I heard another voice from heaven saying, Come out of her (economy) my people, that ye be not partakers of her sins, and that ye receive not of her plagues.

This was true in John's time and its true today this is not just for the tribulation saints.

> 5 For her sins (greedy lust 1 John 2:16-17) have reached up to heaven, and God has remembered her iniquities. (Rev. 18:7)

> 6 Reward her even as she rewarded you, and double unto her double according to her works: in the cup which she hath filled fill to her double.

> 7 How much she hath glorified herself, (lust) and lived deliciously, (greedily) so much torment and sorrow give her: for she sayeth in her heart, I sit a queen; and am no widow, and shall see no sorrow. (poverty, Rev. 18:17)

> 8 Therefore shall her plagues come in one day, death, and mourning and famine; she shall be utterly burned with fire: for strong is the Lord God who judgeth her.

9 And the kings of the earth, who have committed fornication and lived deliciously with her, shall bewail her, and lament for her when they shall see the smoke of her burning,

10 Standing afar off for the fear of her torment, saying, Alas, alas that great city Babylon, that mighty city! for in one hour (a specific period-of time) is thy judgment come.

11 And the merchants of the earth shall weep and mourn over her; for no man buyeth their merchandise anymore:

12 The merchandise of gold, and silver, and precious stones and of pearls, and fine linen, and purple, and silk and scarlet, and all thyine wood, and all manner vessels of ivory, and all manner vessels of most precious wood, and of brass, and iron and marble,

13 And cinnamon and odours, and ointments, and frankincense, and wine, and oil, and fine flower, and wheat, beasts, and sheep, and horses, and chariots, and slaves, and souls of men (mind, will, and emotions) Matthew 22:37

Remember the rider on the black horse in Revelation 6:5-6 famine.

14 And the fruits that thy soul (mind, will, and emotions "lusted") lusted after are departed from thee, and all things which were dainty and goodly are departed from thee, and thou shalt find them no more at all.

15 The merchants of these things, which were made rich by her, shall stand afar off for the fear of her torment, weeping and wailing,

16 And saying, Alas, alas, that great city, that was clothed in fine linen, and purple, and scarlet, (royalty) and decked with gold, and precious stones, and pearls! (wealth)

17 For in one hour so great riches is come to not. (laid waste) And every shipmaster, and all the company in ships, and sailors, and as many as trade by sea, stood afar off,

18 And cried when they saw the smoke of her burning, saying, What city is like unto this great city!

19 And they cast dust on their heads, and cried, weeping and wailing, saying, Alas, alas that great city, (economy) wherein were made rich all that had ships in the sea by reason of her costliness! For in one hour is she made desolate. (sorrow, poverty, Thayer's)

20 Rejoice over her, thou heaven, (Because that is where the resurrected, and raptured saints are.) and ye holy apostles and prophets; for God hath avenged you on her.

John could have written all of chapters 17 and 18 in half the space, but he is making a point of explaining this world's economic system. This cannot be made any clearer.

21 And a mighty angel took up a stone like a great millstone, and cast it into the sea, saying, Thus with

> violence shall that great city Babylon be thrown down, and shall be found no more at all.
>
> 22 And the voice of harpers, and musicians, and of pipers, and trumpeters, shall be heard no more at all in thee; and no craftsman whatsoever craft he be, shall be found any more in thee; and the sound of a millstone shall be heard no more at all in thee;
>
> 23 And the light of the candle shall shine no more at all in thee; and the voice of the bridegroom and of the bride shall be heard no more at all in thee: for thy merchants were the great men of the earth; for by thy sorceries were all nations deceived.
>
> 24 And in her was found the blood of the prophets, and of saints, and all that were slain upon the earth.

In a perfect world we would be under God's love and leadership alone and not under any human or worldly governments economy.

1 John 2:16- 17 For all that is in the world, the lust of the flesh, and the lust of the eyes, and the pride of life, is not of the Father, but is of the world. 17 And the world passeth away, and the lust of it; ...

Revelation Chapter 19:1-10 (mid-tribulation)

19:1-10 is a prophetic scene in heaven which will soon come to pass.

> 1 And after these things I heard a great voice of much people in heaven, saying, Alleluia; Salvation, and glory, and honour, and power, unto the Lord our God:

2 For true and righteous are his judgments: for he hath judged the great whore (the world's economic system), which did corrupt the earth with her fornication, and hath avenged the blood of his servants at her hand.

3 And again they said: Alleluia. And her smoke rose up forever and ever.

4 And the four and the twenty elders fell down and worshiped God, that sat on the throne. saying, Amen; Alleluia.

5 And a voice came from the throne, saying: Praise our God, all ye his servants, and ye that fear (reverence) him, both small and great.

6 And I heard as it were the voice of a great multitude, and as the voice of many waters, (peoples) and (loud) as the voice of mighty thunderings, saying, Alleluia: for the lord God omnipotent reineth.

7 Let us be glad and rejoice, and give honour to him: for the marriage of the Lamb is come, and his wife (holy saints) hath made herself ready.

8 And to her was granted that she should be arrayed in fine linen, clean and white: for the fine linen is the righteousness of the saints.

9 And he, sayeth to me, Write, Blessed are they which are called unto the marriage supper of the Lamb. And he sayeth unto me, these are the true sayings of God.

10 And I fell at his feet to worship him. And he said unto me, See thou do it not: I am thy fellowservant, and of thy brethren that have the testimony of Jesus: worship God: for the testimony of Jesus is the spirit of prophecy.

CHAPTER 6

The Second Half

The seven-year tribulation starts with the rapture of the church of Christ and the resurrection of the bodies of the saints from all time.

And the sealing of the 144,000 apostles in preparation for their three-and-a-half-year ministry.

At mid-tribulation, the 144,000 are raptured and the two olive trees or prophets of Revelation 11:4 and Zechariah 4:3 and 14 begin their ministry in Jerusalem.

Satan is cast down to earth Isaiah 14:12. When Satan is cast down to earth, the man, #666, the antichrist, will become fully possessed by Satan, and he will revoke his treaty. Daniel 9:26-27.

Antichrist will set out to kill the Jews, but God protects them Daniel 12:1, so he turns to the people that have come to faith in Jesus during the tribulation and many will be killed.

He will portray himself as God, and his false prophet will force people to worship him through the mark of the beast.

Together they will set up the abomination that makes desolation, an image of the antichrist on a wing, or corner of the temple and God's holy angels will begin the trumpet judgments working together with the two prophets in Jerusalem. Daniel 9:26-27

From this point forward, we will be moving rapidly from mid-tribulation to the end of the tribulation and the end of the book of Revelation.

The following events occur over the last three-and-a-half years of tribulation which was about the same number of years as the earthly ministry of Jesus, the ministry of the 144,000 during the first half of the tribulation, the Roman destruction of Jerusalem and the second temple, and the worldwide involvement in World Wars I and II. This three-and-a-half year timeline guides us through the book of Revelation.

God has always worked for mankind through mankind. He asked Noah to build an ark, and he did. He asked Abraham to go to the land that he would show him, and he did. He asked Moses to lead Israel out of Egypt, and he did.

But Moses did not work the miracles. God told him what to say and do, and when he did what God said, the angels did the work.

Moses did not kill the first born of the Egyptians, the angel named Death did, and Moses did not part the Red Sea, an angel did.

So, when the two prophets in Jerusalem hear from God, they will speak, and the angels will do the work.

Revelation Chapter 8:2-13

The first four trumpet judgments

> 2 And I saw the seven angels which stood before God; and to them were given seven trumpets.

> 3 And another angel came and stood at the altar, having a golden censer; and there was given unto him much incense, that he should offer it with the prayers of all saints upon the golden altar which was before the throne.

> 4 And the smoke of the incense, which came with the prayers of the saints, ascended up before God out of the angel's hand.

> 5 And the angel took the censer, and filled it with fire of the altar, and cast it into the earth: and there were voices, and thunderings, and lightnings, and an earthquake.

Voices, thunderings, and lightnings proceed from the throne of God. In every case, in Revelation, Rev. 4:5, here in 8:5 and 11:19, this is a prophetic sign in heaven.

> 6 And the seven angels which had the seven trumpets prepared themselves to sound.

> 7 The first angel sounded, the first trumpet and there followed hail and fire (lightning) mingled with blood, and they were (thrown) cast upon the earth: and the third part of the trees was burnt up, and all green grass was burnt up (global impact).

This event is the fulfilment of the prophetic sign in the previous verse 5. The judgments begin with the sounding of the trumpets.

All green grass would include wheat, oats, barley, etc., resulting in famine, which the rider on the black horse symbolizes. Remember, the two prophets in Revelation chapter 11:6 would cause drought by withholding the rain, and they would turn the waters into blood during the three-and-a-half years of their ministry.

Severe drought would cause the vegetation to dry up naturally, that together with supernatural events such as Moses worked through the angels in Egypt at the exodus of Israel explains this judgment well.

Continue Chapter Eight

> 8 And the second angel sounded, the second trumpet and as it were a great mountain (asteroid) burning with fire was cast into the sea: and the third part of the sea became blood; (global impact)

> 9 And the third part of the creatures which were in the sea, and had life, died; and the third part of the ships were destroyed.

One nuclear weapon or a volcano wouldn't kill a third of the life in the sea and wipe out a third of the ships on earth, therefore I believe that this judgment is an asteroid.

> 10 And the third angel sounded, the third trumpet and there fell a great star (asteroid, not a nuclear weapon) from heaven, burning as it were a lamp, and it fell upon the third part of the rivers, and upon the fountains of waters; (global impact)

I believe that the natural world is impacted by spiritual forces or angels along with the natural physical realm. Luke 10:18: And he (Jesus) said unto them, I beheld Satan (an angel) as lightning fall from heaven.

> 11 And the name of the star (possibly angel) is called Wormwood: (a proper name) and the third part of the waters became wormwood; (poisoned) and many men died of the waters, because they were made bitter.

We know from experience that a single nuclear weapon won't poison a third of the fresh water on the earth, but an angel could poison a third of the Earth's fresh water.

> 12 And the fourth angel sounded, the fourth trumpet and the third part of the sun (light) was smitten, and

> the third part of the moon, (light) and the third part of the stars; (light) so as the third part of them was darkened, and the day shone not for a third part of it, and the night likewise.

An asteroid as big as a great mountain would be "white hot" when it hit the sea. One like the one described in verse 8 would cause the atmosphere to be darkened by a third globally just as it is when the sky is overcast regionally.

> 13 And I beheld, and heard an eagle flying through the midst of heaven (sky), saying with a loud voice, Woe, woe, woe, to the inhabiters of the earth, by reason of the other voices of the trumpet of the three angels which are yet to sound!

The trumpet sounds of the fifth, sixth and seventh angels are the three woes and is in part how we know that these trumpet judgments occur toward the end of the tribulation, they occur rather quickly one after another and take us to Armageddon.

Revelation Chapter 9

The first woe

> 1 And the fifth angel sounded, the fifth trumpet and I saw a star (angel) fall from heaven unto the earth: and to him was given the key of the bottomless pit.

Jesus has the keys. Revelation 1:18, says he holds the key to the bottomless pit the prison for the demons and the key of death.

This star or angel in verse 1 fell from the sky to the earth or from the first heaven to earth and was given a key.

Vine's describes as many as five heavens. I believe that the heavens can be summed up in three:

The first heaven is our atmosphere the second is the stellar heavens where the stars are, and God's heaven of heavens is the third heaven

For reference, Paul wrote of having been caught up to God's heaven in 2 Corinthians 12:2 … such an one caught up to the third heaven.

Revelation 9:1 is confirmed in Revelation 12:7-9

> 7 And there was war in heaven: Michael and his angels fought against the dragon; and the dragon fought and his angels,
>
> 8 And prevailed not; neither was their place found anymore in heaven.
>
> 9 And the great dragon was cast out, that old serpent, called the Devil, and Satan, which deceiveth the whole world: he was cast out into the earth, and his angels were cast out with him. Satan and his angels would have been cast out prior to the first trumpet.

Chapter 9 continues

> 9:2 And he (the fallen angel) opened the bottomless pit; (hell or really Tartarus) and there arose a smoak out of the pit, as the smoke from a great furnace; and the sun and the air were darkened by reason of the smoke of the pit. (2 Peter 2:4)

Hell, or Tartarus, is opened, and the demons of hell are released upon the earth.

> Jude 1:6, And the angels which kept not their first estate, but left their own habitation, he hath reserved

in everlasting chains under darkness unto the judgment of the great day. See 2 Peter 2:4

3 And there came out of the smoke (not hell) locust (instruments of war, see the following verses 7-10) upon the earth: and unto them was given power, as the scorpions of the earth have power.

Over a fourth part of the earth. Revelation 6:8

4 And it was commanded them that they should not harm the grass of the earth, neither any green thing, neither any tree; (a third of the trees and all the green grass was already burned up Ch. 8:7) but (hurt) only those men which have not the seal of God in their foreheads.

The tribulation saints are protected from God's judgments on the ungodly.

Those who come to Messiah, Christ Jesus, during the tribulation are protected from God's judgments but not from the antichrist, unless you are a faithful Jew in Israel.

5 And to them it was given that they should not kill them, but that they should be tormented five months: and their torment was as the torment of a scorpion, when it striketh a man.

6 And in those days shall men seek death, and shall not find it; and shall desire to die, and death shall flee from them.

7 And the shapes of the locusts were like unto horses prepared unto battle; (instruments of war) and on their heads were as it were crowns like gold, and their faces were as the faces of men.

These are probably drones or helicopters spraying chemical agents.

> 8 And they had hair as the hair of a woman, and their teeth were as the teeth of lions (firepower).
>
> 9 And they had breastplates (armor), as it were breastplates of iron; and the sound of their wings was as the sound of chariots of many horses running to battle.
>
> 10 And they had tails like unto scorpions, and there were stings in their tails: and their power was to hurt men five months.
>
> 11 They had a king over them, which is the angel of the bottomless pit, whose name in the Hebrew tongue is Abaddon, but in the Greek tongue hath his name Apollyon (destroyer).
>
> 12 (The second woe) One woe is past; and, behold, there come two woes more thereafter.
>
> 13 And the sixth angel sounded, the sixth trumpet and I heard a voice from the four horns of the golden alter which is before God,
>
> 14 Saying to the sixth angel which had the trumpet, Loose the four angels (four horsemen) which are bound in the great river Euphrates.

This area of the Middle East would be the epicenter of the war of the fourth part of the earth.

Revelation 6:8:

> 8 And I looked, and behold a pale horse: and his name that sat on him was Death, and Hell followed with him. And power was given unto them (the four horsemen) over the fourth part of the earth, to kill with sword (red horse), and with hunger, and with death (black horse), and with the beasts of the earth (pale horse).

The rider on the white horse of Revelation Chapter 6 sets up the geo-political conditions in the hearts and minds of men in political power.

Chapter Nine continues

> 15 And the four angels (or horsemen) were loosed, which were prepared for an hour, and a day, and a month, and a year, (kept for a specific time) for to slay the third part of men.

> Revelation 7:1-2

> 1 And after these things I saw four angels standing on the four corners of the earth, holding the four winds (spirits) of the earth,

> 2 that the wind should not blow (bring judgment, for a time) on the earth, nor on the sea, nor on any tree.

This coming judgment of war has global impact and will affect the whole world, but the battlefields cover only a fourth of the land mass of the earth.

A third of mankind on the earth will be killed by the red horse, War. So this might be where the nukes come out.

> 9:16 And the number of the army of horsemen (troops) were two hundred thousand thousand: and I heard the number of them.

This number is the total number of troops going to war, not only the ones that might come from the "kings of the east."

This war is not Armageddon. The antichrist will not have the support of all nations, because many will be at war with him,

See Daniel 8:23-26, 9:26-27 and 11:41.

> 17 And thus I saw the horses in the vision, and them that sat on them, having breast plates of fire, (red) jacinth, (dark blue) and brimstone: (yellow) the heads of the horses were as the heads of lions; (fierce) and out of their mouths issued fire, smoke and brimstone. (sulfur, gun powder)

> 18 By these three was a third part of men killed by the fire, and by the smoke, and by the brimstone, (sulfur, gun powder) that issued out of their mouths. (Gun barrels and canons or nuclear silos perhaps).

> 19 For their power is in their mouth, and in their tails: for their tails were like unto serpents, and had heads, and with them they do hurt.

Much like the locust in the first woe, here in this second woe.

> 20 And the rest of men which were not killed by these plagues yet repented not of the works of their hands,

The rider on the white horse from Revelation chapter six is the influencing spirit.

Verse 20 continues,

> 20 that they should not worship devils, and idols of gold, and silver, and brass, and stone, and of wood: which neither can see, nor hear, nor walk:

> 21 Neither repented they of their murders, nor their sorceries, their fornication, nor their thefts.

Revelation Chapter 10

A prophetic sign

This prophesy is given earlier in mid-tribulation, I put the scripture here to tie this to the two halves of Chapter 11 as follows.

> 1 And I saw another mighty angel come down from heaven, clothed with a cloud (of glory): and a rainbow was upon his head, and his face was as it were the sun, and his feet as pillars of fire:

This angel or messenger is Jesus. See Revelation Chapters 1:7 and 14:14-15.

> 2 And he had in his hand a little book open: and he set his right foot upon the sea (the nations) and his left foot on the earth (the land of Jacob, Israel),

Why would one foot on the sea and one on the land represent Jesus standing on the nations and on Israel?

Revelation 17:15: The waters which you saw are peoples and multitudes, and nations and languages.

Now we know what the water represents, so can we speculate that the land is Israel?

I think so. These symbols aren't in here for no reason. They must have a meaning, and I believe that we should explore them.

The tribulation is the last week of years appointed to Israel. This is the time of Jacob's trouble, and Messiah Jesus is coming back for the Israel that rejected him, and he's coming back to Jerusalem in the land of Israel where his prophets Enoch and Elijah are.

Thayer's Lexicon coded to *Strong's*, 1093 a country, ... land ... within fixed boundaries, ... when it is plain from the context what land is meant, as that of the Jews: Lk. 21:23, Ro.9:28, Jas. 5:17; there you have the answer.

Revelation Ch. 10 continues

> 3 And cried with a loud voice, as when a lion roareth: (the Lion of the tribe of Judah) and when he cried, seven thunders, uttered their voices.

> 4 And when the seven thunders uttered their voices, I was about to write: and I heard a voice from heaven saying unto me, Seal up those things which the seven thunders have uttered, and write them not.

This is one of the few mysteries in the book of Revelation.

> 5 And the angel which I saw stand upon the sea and on the earth lifted up his hand to heaven, ('since he could swear by no higher, he swore by himself,' found in some translations)

> 6 And sware by him that liveth forever and ever, who created heaven and the things that therein are, and the earth, and the things that therein are, and in the sea, and the things that are therein, that there should be time no longer:

> 7 But in the days of the voice (trumpet) of the seventh angel, when he shall begin to sound, the mystery of God should be finished, as he hath declared to his servants the prophets.

> 8 And the voice which I heard from heaven spake unto me again, and said, Go, and take the little book which is open in the hand of the angel which standeth upon the sea and upon the earth.
>
> 9 And I went unto the angel and said unto him, Give me the little book. And he said unto me, Take it, and eat it up; and it shall make thy belly bitter, but it shall be in thy mouth sweet as honey.
>
> 10 And I took the little book from the angel's hand, and ate it up; it was in my mouth sweet as honey: and as soon as I had eaten it, my belly was bitter.
>
> 11 And he said unto me, Thou must prophesy again before many peoples, and nations, and tongues, and kings.

This prophecy is found here in the first six verses of Revelation 11, which is mid-tribulation, but the second half of chapter 11 takes us to the end of the tribulation.

> 1 And there was given me a reed like unto a rod: and the angel stood, saying, Rise, and measure the temple of God, and the alter, and them that worship therein.
>
> 2 But the court, which is without the temple leave out, and measure it not; for it is given unto the Gentiles: and the holy city (Jerusalem) shall they tread under foot forty and two months. (3.5-years)
>
> 3 And I will give power unto my two witnesses, and they shall prophesy a thousand two hundred and three score days (the second half of the tribulation), clothed in sackcloth.

> 4 These are the two olive trees, and the two candlesticks (Prophets, the light of God to Israel as in the days prior to the church.) standing before the God of the earth.

> 5 And if any man wants to hurt them, fire proceedeth out of their mouth, and devoureth their enemies: and if any man will hurt them, he must in this manner be killed.

> 6 These have power to shut heaven, that it rain not in the days of their prophecy: and have power over the waters to turn them to blood, and to smite the earth with all plagues, as often as they will.

Can you see how the angels with the trumpets of judgment line up with the two prophets? Now we are going back to the two olive trees.

There is incredibly good reason to believe that they are Enoch and Elijah. Beside the fact that neither one died a physical death, Enoch represents the wild olive, Gentiles, and Elijah represents the cultured olive, Israel.

Romans 11:24: For if thou wert cut out of an olive tree which is wild by nature, (Gentiles) and wert grafted contrary to nature into a good olive tree: (Israel) how much more shall these, which be the natural branches, (Israel) be grafted (back) into their own olive tree? (See also Zechariah 4:12-14)

CHAPTER 7

The Final Days

Revelation Chapter 11:7-19

Satan and the antichrist are finally allowed to kill the two prophets, this event gives God another opportunity to save lost people.

After three-and-a-half days, God raises them and snatches them up to heaven.

Within the hour, an earthquake strikes Jerusalem and seven thousand people die but the survivors recognize God and give glory to him, thus bringing salvation to them.

> 11:7 And when they shall have finished their testimony the beast that ascendeth out of the bottomless pit shall make war against them, and overcome them, and kill them.
>
> 8 And their dead bodies shall lie in the street of the great city, which spiritually is called Sodom and Egypt, were also our Lord was crucified.
>
> 9 And they of the people and kindreds and tongues and nations shall see their dead bodies three days and an

> half, and shall not suffer (allow) their dead bodies to be put into graves.
>
> 10 And they (the ungodly) that dwell upon the earth shall rejoice over them, and make merry, and send gifts one to another; because these two prophets tormented (through angels) them that dwell on the earth.
>
> 11 And after three days and an half the Spirit of life from God entered into them, and they stood upon their feet; and great fear fell upon them which saw them.

By now Moses has been dead for about thirty-five hundred years, his body has already been resurrected at the pre-tribulation resurrection, rapture.

Charles Capps teaches about the body of Moses having been raised and caught up along with the rapture of Elijah, which I believe to be true.

The Lord God Almighty could send him back, but I believe that he will send Enoch and Elijah as the two prophets.

From the scriptures, I don't believe that a resurrected body can ever be killed or die again.

> 9:12 And they heard a great voice from heaven saying unto them, Come up hither. And they ascended up to heaven in a cloud; and their enemies beheld them.
>
> 13 And the same hour was there a great earthquake, and the tenth part of the city (Jerusalem) fell, and in the earthquake were slain of men seven thousand: and the remnant were affrighted, and gave glory to the God of heaven.

These survivors have not received the mark of the beast, and they give glory to God.

During the seven bowl judgments of God's wrath, no one repents and gives God any glory. This was the last opportunity to escape the wrath to come.

The sixth trumpet of Revelation chapter 9:13 was the second woe, the war that kills a third of mankind over an area of one quarter of the earth.

Revelation 10:7: But in the days of the voice (trumpet) of the seventh angel, when he shall begin to sound, the mystery of God should be finished, as he hath declared to his servants the prophets.

These are those days and they are described in the next six verses of Revelation chapter 11:

> 14 The second woe is passed (the sixth trumpet); and behold the third woe cometh quickly.
>
> 15 And the seventh angel sounded (his trumpet); and there were great voices in heaven, saying, The kingdoms of this world are become the kingdoms of our Lord, and of his Christ; and he shall rein forever and ever.
>
> 16 And the four and twenty elders, which sat before God on their seats, fell upon their faces, and worshiped God,
>
> 17 Saying, We give thee thanks, O Lord God Almighty, which art, and wast, and art to come; because thou hast taken to thee thy great power, and hast reigned.
>
> 18 And the nations were angry, and thy wrath is come, and the time of the dead, (spiritually dead) that they should be judged, and that thou shouldest give reward unto your servants the prophets, and to the saints, and

> them that fear thy name, small and great; and shouldest destroy them which destroy the earth.
>
> 19 And the temple of God was opened in heaven, (to rapture the tribulation saints) and there was seen in his temple the ark of his testament: and there were lightnings, and voices, and thunderings, and an earthquake and great hail.

This is a prophetic scene in heaven

Revelation Chapter 14:14-20 is also a prophetic vision

The scriptures that follow will help clarify the prophecy and set the stage and then the chapter will follow.

Chapter 14:14-20 ties the resurrection and rapture of the two prophets or olive trees and the rapture of the tribulation saints together.

These scriptures can be a little difficult to understand depending on the Bible translation you read. so I use several and a good concordance to get the best translation.

We must rely on the Holy Spirit to get the interpretation and the context of the text.

The Bible bears witness to itself, so somewhere in the Bible there is an answer to a difficult mystery.

Jesus explains the mystery of the wheat and the tares (weeds) in Matthew 13:36-43

> 36 Then Jesus sent the multitude away, and went into the house: and his disciples came unto him, saying, Declare unto us the parable of the tares of the field.
>
> 37 He answered and said unto them, He that soweth the good seed (gospel of grace) is the Son of man;
>
> 38 The field is the world; the good seed are the children of the kingdom; but the tares are the (unbelieving) children of the wicked one.

> 39 The enemy that sowed (planted) them is the devil; the harvest is the end of the world; and the reapers are the angels.
>
> 40 As therefore the tares (weeds) are gathered and burned in the fire; so shall it be in the end of this world.
>
> 41 The Son of man shall send forth his angels, and they shall gather out of his kingdom all things that offend, and them which do iniquity;
>
> 42 And shall cast them into a furnace (lake) of fire: there shall be wailing and gnashing of teeth.
>
> 43 Then shall the righteous (in Messiah Jesus) shine forth as the sun in the kingdom of their Father. Who hath ears to hear, let him hear.

Please bear with me, this will be made relevant in the verses that follow.

Revelation Chapter 14:14-20

> 14 And I looked, and behold a white cloud, (of saints) and upon the cloud one sat like unto the Son of man having on his head a golden crown, and in his hand a sharp sickle.

This is a prophetic scene in heaven, here we see the Lord seated upon the mount of the congregation.

Mystery Babylon the world's economic system sat upon the beast, the last earthly kingdom Revelation 17:3 &15 and 18, peoples, nations and kings.

> 15 And another angel came out of the temple, crying with a loud voice to him (Jesus) that sat on the cloud,

> Thrust in thy sickle, and reap: for the time is come for thee to reap: for the harvest of the earth is ripe.

> 16 And he that sat on the cloud thrust in his sickle on the earth; and the earth was reaped (harvested).

This harvest of the earth is the harvest of the wheat, and is the prophetic pre-wrath rapture of the tribulation saints.

Next is the harvest of the weeds to be burned in the lake of fire.

> 17 And another angel came out of the temple which is in heaven, he also having a sharp sickle. (not sitting on a cloud)

> 18 And another angel came out from the alter, which had power over fire; (to burn the tares) and cried with a loud cry to him that had the sharp sickle, saying, Thrust in thy sharp sickle, and gather the clusters of the vine of the earth; for her grapes are fully ripe.

> 19 And the angel thrust in his sickle into the earth and harvested the grapevine of the earth and threw them into the great wine press of the wrath of God.

> 20 And the winepress was trodden without the city, (Jerusalem) and blood came out of the winepress, even unto the horse bridles, by the space of a thousand and six hundred furlongs. Or about two hundred miles, at Armageddon

The grapes that are crushed represent the pouring out of blood, they are also the tares or weeds who are the wicked ones to be burned forever in the eternal lake of fire.

So what can we learn from the parable of the wheat and the tares in Matthew 13:24-30?

We will skip to v. 30: Let both grow together until the harvest: and in the time of harvest I will say to the reapers (angels), Gather ye together first the tares, and bind them in bundles, to burn them: but gather the wheat into my barn.

God loves everybody and does not want to lose anyone, so he spares the weeds until the very end.

Then he will send his angels to gather his own, the wheat and spare them from the destruction that is coming.

The gathering of the wheat is the catching away of the tribulation saints in the next chapter.

Revelation Chapter Fifteen

The rapture of the tribulation saints

Now we see in heaven the tribulation saints snatched from the earth this time just prior to God pouring out his wrath on the wicked of the world.

They are standing beside the river of life in the throne room of God and he has given them harps, and they sing songs of praise and victory.

They had not taken the mark of the beast, and they were not martyred but were delivered.

The martyred saints of the tribulation go straight to heaven as disembodied souls each one as they are killed. Revelation 6:9

The pre-wrath raptured saints sing the songs of Moses and the Lamb because they had been delivered through the tribulation somewhat like Israel was delivered from the death angel and through the Red Sea and they are delivered from the wrath of God to come.

> 15:1 And I saw another sign in heaven, great and marvelous, seven angels having the seven last plagues: for in them is filled up the wrath of God.

> 2 And I saw as it were a sea of glass (the river of life, which is before the throne) mingled with fire (Holy Spirit): and them that had gotten the victory over the beast, and over his image, and over his mark, and over the number of his name, stand on the sea of glass (in heaven), having the harps of God.

They are right there in the throne room of God, in heaven and have the harps of God.

> 3 And they sing the song of Moses (Exodus 15:1-21) the servant of God, and the song of the Lamb, saying, Great and marvelous are thy works, Lord God Almighty; just and true are thy ways, thou King of saints.

> 4 Who shall not fear thee, O Lord, and glorify thy name? for thou only art holy: for all nations shall come and worship before thee; for thy judgments are made manifest (Judgment of deliverance in this case).

> 5 And after that (the rapture of the tribulation saints), I looked, and, behold the temple of the tabernacle of the Testimony in heaven was opened (to let the seven angels of wrath out):

> 6 And the seven angels came out of the temple, having the seven plagues, clothed in pure and white linen, and having their breasts girded with golden girdles (vests).

> 7 And one of the four beasts (cherubs) gave unto the seven angels seven golden vials full of the wrath of God, who liveth forever and ever.

> 8 And the temple was filled with (a cloud of) smoke from the glory of God, and from his power; and no

> man was able to enter into the temple till the seven plagues of the seven angels were fulfilled.

Now no man was able to enter into the temple because heaven is closed once again until the wrath of God is completed.

Revelation Chapter Sixteen

The third woe, the seventh trumpet from Rev.11:15

Revelation 11:15-19 the sounding of the seventh angel begins the wrath of God and of the Lamb as seen here.

> 16:1 And I heard a great voice out of the temple saying to the seven angels, Go your ways, and pour out the vials of the wrath of God upon the earth.

> 2 And the first went, and poured out his vial upon the earth; and there fell a noisome and grievous sore upon the men which had the mark of the beast, and upon them which worshiped his image.

Not all people around the world will take the mark of the beast, perhaps even some unbelievers.

Remember the faithful Jews of Israel, the descendants of Jacob, are still hidden away in the wilderness protected by God.

Daniel 12:12: Blessed is he who waits and comes to 1,335 days.

> 16:3 And the second angel poured out his vial upon the sea; and it became as the blood of a dead man: and every living soul died in the sea.

Vine's, SOUL (d) the seat of personality, Luke 9:25 … (e) … that by which he perceives, reflects, feels, desires, …(f) the seat of will and purpose, Matthew 22:37

4 And the third angel poured out his vial upon the rivers and fountains of waters; and they became blood.

5 And I heard the angel of the waters say, Thou art righteous, O Lord, which art and wast, and shalt be, because thou hast judged thus.

6 For they have shed the blood of saints and prophets, and thou hast given them blood to drink; for they are worthy.

7 And I heard another out of the alter say, even so, Lord God Almighty, true and righteous are your judgments. (of blessing and cursing)

8 And the fourth angel poured out his vial upon the sun; and power was given unto him to scorch men with fire.

9 And men were scorched with great heat, and blasphemed the name of God, which hath power over these plagues: and repented they not to give him glory.

10 And the fifth angel poured out his vial upon the seat of the beast; and his kingdom was full of darkness; and they gnawed their tongues for pain,

11 And blasphemed the God of heaven because of their pains and their sores, and repented not of their deeds.

12 And the sixth angel poured out his vial upon the great river Euphrates; and the waters thereof was dried up, that the way of the kings from the east might be prepared.

13 And I saw three unclean spirits like frogs come out of the mouth of the dragon, and out of the mouth of the beast, and out of the mouth of the false prophet.

14 For they are the spirits of devils, working miracles, which go forth unto the kings of the earth (not just from the east) and of the whole world, to gather them to the battle on the great day of God Almighty.

15 Behold, I come as a thief. (salvation scripture) Blessed is he that watcheth, and keepeth his garments, lest he walk naked, and they see his shame.

16 And he gathered them to a place called in the Hebrew tongue Armageddon.

17 And the seventh angel poured out his vial into the air; and there came a great voice out of the temple of heaven, from the throne, saying, it is done.

18 And there were voices, and thunders, and lightnings; and there was a great earthquake, such as was not since men were upon the earth, so mighty an earthquake, and so great.

The prophetic signs in heaven are now fulfilled.

19 And the great city was divided into three parts, and the cities of the nations fell: and great Babylon came in remembrance before God, to give unto her the cup of the wine of the fierceness of his wrath.

20 And every island fled away, and the mountains were not found.

21 And there fell upon men a great hail out of heaven, every stone about the weight of a talent (a hundred pounds): and men blasphemed God because of the plague of the hail; for the plague thereof was exceeding great.

REVELATION CHAPTER 19:11-21

11 And I saw heaven opened (to let out the army of heaven), and behold a white horse; and he that sat upon him was called Faithful and True, and in righteousness he doth judge and make war.

12 His eyes were as flame of fire, and on his head were many crowns; and he had a name written, that no one knew, but he himself.

13 And he was clothed with a vesture dipped in blood: his name is called The Word of God.

14 And the armies which were in heaven followed him (the resurrected and raptured saints) upon white horses, clothed in fine linen, white and clean.

Fine linen is the righteousness of the saints.

15 And out of his mouth goeth a sharp sword, that with it he should smite the nations: and he shall rule them with a rod of iron: (Rev. 12:14.) and he treadeth the winepress (Rev. 14:20) of the fierceness and wrath of Almighty God.

16 And he hath on his vesture and on his thigh, he has this name written, KING OF KINGS AND LORD OF LORDS.

17 And I saw an angel standing in the sun (sky); and he cried with a loud voice, saying to all the fowls that fly in the midst of heaven (sky), Come and gather yourselves together unto the supper of the great God;

18 That ye may eat the flesh of kings, and the flesh of captains, and the flesh of mighty men, and the flesh of horses, and them that sit on them, and the flesh of all men, both free and bond, both small and great.

19 And I saw the beast, and the kings of the earth (not just the kings of the east), and their armies, gathered together to make war against him that sat on the horse and against his army.

20 And the beast was taken, and with him the false prophet that wrought miracles before him, with which he deceived them that have received the mark of the beast, and them that worshiped his image, These both were cast alive into the lake of fire burning with brimstone.

21 And the remnant were slain with the sword of him that sat upon the horse, which sword proceeded out of his mouth (spoken word): and all the fowls were filled with their flesh. Armageddon

I must put parts of the following prophesy in here for a couple of reasons; one is that a lot of commentators, theologians, and preachers say that the war of Gog and Magog recorded in Ezekiel 38 and 39 must happen prior to the tribulation or the rapture of the church or perhaps at about that time.

But the battle of Armageddon at the end of the tribulation is the war of Ezekiel 38 and 39 and confirms and witnesses to the previous chapters Revelation 16, 14:14-20 and 19:11-21 also as Jesus said in Matthew 24:21-31.

You can find more supporting scriptures in Zechariah 12:1-4 and 14:1-9, among others.

Again, because there is a lot of misunderstanding of Ezekiel 38 and 39, I chose to add here some of Ezekiel Chapter 38 and 39:

Ezekiel Chapter 38

> 17 Thus sayeth the Lord GOD; Art thou he of whom I have spoken in old time by my servants the prophets of Israel, which prophesied in those days many years that I would bring thee against them?

> 18 And it shall come to pass at the same time when Gog shall come against the land of Israel, saith the Lord GOD, that my fury shall come up in my face.

> 19 For in my jealousy and in the fire of my wrath I have spoken, that in that day (of wrath) there shall be a great shaking (earthquake) in the land of Israel;

> 20 So that the fishes of the sea, the fowls of the heaven, and the beasts of the field, and all creeping things that creep upon the earth, and all the men that are upon the face of the earth shall shake at my presence, and the mountains shall be thrown down, and the steep places shall fall, and every wall shall fall to the ground.

> 21 And I will call for a sword against him (Gog) throughout all my holy mountains, sayeth the Lord GOD: every man's sword shall be against his brother.

22 And I will plead (speak) against him with pestilence and with blood; and I will rain upon him, and upon his bands, an overflowing rain, great hailstones, fire and brimstone.

23 Thus I will magnify myself, and sanctify myself; and I will be known in the eyes of many nations, and they shall know that I am the LORD.

Ezekiel Chapter 39

4 Thou shalt fall upon the mountains of Israel, thou, and all thy bands, and the people that is with thee: I will give thee unto the ravenous birds of every sort, and to the beasts (wild animals) of the field to be devoured.

7 So will I make my holy name known in the midst of my people Israel; and I will not let them pollute my holy name anymore: and the heathen (ungodly) shall know that I am the LORD, the Holy One in Israel.

8 Behold it is come, and it is done, (Revelation 6:17) saith the Lord GOD; this is the day whereof I have spoken.

13 Yea, all the people of the land (of Israel) shall bury them; and it shall be to them a renown the day (one specific day) that I shall be glorified, saith the Lord GOD.

20 Thus ye shall be filled at my table with horses and chariots, (implements of war) with mighty men, and with all the men of war, saith the Lord GOD.

> 22 So the house of Israel will know that I am the LORD their God from that day forward.

The war of Ezekiel 38 and 39 and the battle of Armageddon are one and the same. The details are unmistakable. Look at the previous verse 22: From that day forward the house of Israel will know that I am the Lord their God.

This cannot happen until the end of the tribulation and it will only happen once.

Compare Revelation 19:17: An angel calls out to all the birds, come gather together for the great supper of God, and Ezekiel 39:4 and 20: I will give you to birds of every sort, and to the wild animals, to be eaten. v. 20, at my table you will be filled ...

Revelation 16:16 he gathered them at Armageddon and in vv. 20-21, there is great hail and an earthquake. In Revelation 19:11-21, we see Armageddon, and this great conflict matches the signs, symbols, and events in Ezekiel 38 and 39.

The descendants of Jacob, Israel will come back to bury the dead and burn the implements of war left behind in Ezekiel 39:9-11.

The armies of the world come to Israel to fight the antichrist and his armies, but they all turn to fight against the Lord and his army as he appears.

CHAPTER 8

The One Thousand Year Rule of Christ

Jesus will live on earth with the saints from the beginning of time, including the ones that came to faith in Jesus and those who were killed during the tribulation. They will be resurrected.

Only those who had received the mark of the beast and the warring invaders of Israel at the battle of Armageddon will be slain when Jesus speaks the word, then the angels will do the work.

All the people who survive the tribulation will live long lives and repopulate the earth while Satan is bound in hell for a thousand years.

Revelation Chapter Twenty

> 1 And I saw an angel come down from heaven, having the key of the bottomless pit (Tartarus) and a great chain in his hand.

> 2 And he laid hold on the dragon, that old serpent, which is the Devil, and Satan, and bound him a thousand years,

3 And cast him into the bottomless pit, and shut him up, and set a seal upon him, that he should deceive the nations no more, till the thousand years should be fulfilled: and after that he must be loosed a little season.

4 And I saw thrones, and they that sat upon them (the saints), and judgment was given unto them: and I saw the souls of them that were beheaded (Revelation 6:9) for the witness of Jesus, and for the word of God, and which had not worshiped the beast, neither his image, neither received his mark upon their foreheads or their hands; (those believers who were killed during the tribulation) and they lived (again) and reined with Christ a thousand years.

5 But the rest of the dead (all the unbelievers who have died since Adam) lived not again until the thousand years were finished. This is the first resurrection.

The first resurrection here is the completion of the first which began with the resurrection of Jesus and many saints.

Matthew 27:52-53: And the graves were opened; and many bodies of the saints which slept arose, And came out of the graves after his resurrection, and went into the holy city, and appeared unto many.

Then the pre-tribulation resurrection rapture is foretold in 1Corinthians 15:51-53: Behold I shew you a mystery; We shall not all sleep, but we shall be changed, In a moment, in the twinkling of an eye, at the last trump: for the trumpet shall sound, and the dead shall be raised incorruptible, and we shall be changed. For this … mortal must put on immortality. So … Death is swallowed up in victory.

And in 2 Thessalonians 2:1, 1 Thessalonians 4:13-18, and then the resurrection and rapture as it actually happens in Revelation chapter 7:9-17.

Then the mid-tribulation rapture of the 144,000 happens in Revelation 14:1-5: And I looked, and lo, a Lamb stood on the mount Sion, and with him an hundred forty and four thousand, … This is the heavenly mount Sion; Jesus doesn't set foot on earth until Armageddon.

Verse 2 … And I heard a voice from heaven, … and I heard the voice of harpers harping with their harps: 3 And they (the 144,000) sung as it were a new song before the throne, … and no man could learn that song but the hundred and forty and four thousand, which were redeemed from the earth. Verse 4 … These were redeemed from among men, … and verse 5 … they are without fault before the throne of God.

And then the pre-day of wrath rapture of the tribulation saints in Revelation 15:1-3: And I saw another sign in heaven, great and marvelous, seven angels having the seven last plagues: Verse 2: And I saw … them that had gotten the victory over the beast, … stand on the sea of glass, having the harps of God. Verse 3: and they sing the song of Moses … and the song of the lamb, etc.

And the two olive trees resurrection, rapture as seen in Revelation 11:12.

> 20:6 Blessed and holy is he that hath part in the first resurrection: on such the second death hath no power, but they shall be priest of God and of Christ, and shall rein with him a thousand years.
>
> 7 And when the thousand years are expired, Satan shall be loosed out of his prison,
>
> 8 And shall go out to deceive the nations (some who are born during the thousand years) which are in the four quarters of the earth, Gog and Magog, to gather them together to battle: the number of whom is as the sand of the sea.

Is this Gog and Magog Russia? I think not.

9 And they went up on the breadth of the earth, and compassed the camp of the saints about, and the beloved city: and fire came (swiftly) down from God out of heaven, and devoured them.

10 And the devil, that deceived them was cast into the lake of fire and brimstone, where the beast and the false prophet are, and shall be tormented day and night (alive) for ever and ever.

11 And I saw a great white throne, and him (Jesus) that sat on it, from whose face the earth and the heaven fled away; and there was found no place for them.

12 And I saw the (spiritually) dead small and great, stand before God; and the books were opened: (books of works) another book (singular) was opened, which is the book of life: and the dead were judged out of those things written in the books, according to their works.

13 And the sea gave up the dead (bodies) which were in it; and death and hell delivered up the dead (spirits) which were in them: (resurrected) and they were judged every man according to their works.

14 And death and hell (Hades) were cast into the lake of fire. This is the second death.

There will be no more death nor hell so no one will spend eternity in hell but rather in THE LAKE OF FIRE, the second death which is exile from God.

15 And whosoever was not found written in the book of life was cast into the lake of fire. Where they will live forever, Mark 9:46.

Revelation Chapter Twenty-one

1 And I saw a new heaven and a new earth: for the first heaven and the first earth were passed away; and there was no more sea (great ocean).

Revelation 20:11 Earth and heaven fled from his presence, and there was found no place for them.

The heavens and earth will be recreated.

2 And I John, saw the holy city, new Jerusalem, coming down from God out of heaven, prepared as a bride adorned for her husband.

3 And I heard a great voice out of heaven saying, Behold the tabernacle (home) of God is with men, and he will dwell with them, they shall be his people, and God himself shall be with them, and be their God.

4 And God shall wipe away all tears from their eyes; and there shall be no more death, neither sorrow, nor crying, neither shall there be any more pain: for the former things are passed away.

5 And he that sat upon the throne said, Behold, I make all things new. And he said unto me, Write, for these words are true and faithful.

6 And he said unto me, It is done. I am Alpha and Omega, the beginning and the end. I will give unto him that is athirst of the fountain of the water of life freely. (salvation scripture)

7 He that overcometh (all believers are overcomers) shall inherit all things; and I will be his God, and he shall be my son.

8 But the fearful, and unbelieving, and the abominable, and murderers, and whoremongers, and sorcerers, and idolaters, and all liars, shall have their part in the lake which burneth with fire and brimstone: which is the second death.

9 And there came unto me one of the seven angels which had the seven vials full of the seven last plagues, and talked with me, saying, Come hither, I will shew thee the bride, the Lamb's wife.

The church is wed with the kingdom.

10 And he carried me away in the spirit to a great and high mountain, (Kingdom) and shewed me that great City, the holy Jerusalem, descending out of heaven from God,

11 Having the glory of God: and her light was like unto a stone most precious, even like a jasper stone, clear as crystal;

12 And had a wall great and high, and had twelve gates, and at the gates twelve angels, and names written thereon, which are the names of the twelve tribes (elders) of the children of Israel:

13 On the east three gates; on the north three gates; on the south three gates; and on the west three gates.

14 And the wall of the city had twelve foundations, and in them the names of the twelve apostles (elders) of the Lamb.

15 And he that talked with me had a golden reed to measure the city, and the gates thereof, and the wall thereof.

16 And the city lieth foursquare, and the length is as large as the breadth: and he measured the city with the reed, twelve thousand furlongs. (about 1,400 miles) The length, and the breadth and the height of it are equal.

17 And he measured the wall thereof, an hundred and forty and four cubits, (about 200 feet thick) according to the measure of a man, that is, of the angel.

18 And the building of the wall of it was of jasper: and the city was pure gold, like unto clear glass.

19 And the foundations of the wall of the city were garnished with all manner of precious stones. The first foundation was jasper; the second, sapphire; the third, a chalcedony; the fourth, an emerald;

20 The fifth, sardonyx; the sixth, sardius; the seventh, chrysolite; the eighth, beryl; the nineth, topaz; the tenth, chrysoprasus; the eleventh, jacinth; the twelfth, an amethyst.

21 And the twelve gates were twelve pearls; every several gate was of one pearl: and the street of the city was pure gold, as it were transparent glass.

22 And I saw no temple therein: for the Lord God Almighty and the Lamb are the temple of it.

23 And the city had no need of the sun, neither of the moon, to shine in it: for the glory of God did lighten it, and the Lamb is the light thereof.

24 And the nations of them which are saved shall walk in the light of it: and the kings of the earth do bring their glory and honour into it.

25 And the gates of it shall not be shut at all by day: for there shall be no night there.

26 And they shall bring the glory and honour of the nations into it.

27 But there shall in no wise enter into it anything that defileth, neither whatsoever worketh abomination, or maketh a lie: but they which are written in the Lamb's book of life.

Revelation Chapter Twenty-two

1 And he shewed me a pure river of water of life, as clear as crystal, proceeding (flowing) out of the throne of God and of the Lamb.

2 In the midst of the street of it, and on either side of the river, (of life) was there the tree of life, which bare twelve manner of fruits, and yielded her fruit every month: and the leaves of the tree were for the healing of the nations.

3 And there shall be no more curse: but the throne of God and of the Lamb shall be in it; and his servants shall serve him:

4 And they (the saints) shall see his face; and his name shall be in their foreheads.

5 And there shall be no night there; and they need no candle, neither the light of the sun; for the Lord God giveth them light: and they shall rein forever and ever.

6 And he said unto me, These sayings are faithful and true: and the Lord God of the holy prophets sent his angel to shew unto his servants the things which must shortly be done.

7 Behold, I (Jesus) come quickly: blessed is he that keepeth the sayings of the prophesy of this book. (of Revelation)

8 And I John saw these things, and heard them. And when I had heard and seen, I fell down to worship before the feet of the angel (one of the seven) which shewed me these things.

9 Then saith he unto me, See thou do it not: for I am thy fellowservant, and of thy brethren the prophets, and of them which keep the words of this book: worship God.

10 And he saith unto me, seal not the sayings of the prophecy of this book: for the time is at hand.

Unlike (Daniel 12:4) this book isn't to be sealed up, but taught and understood therefore its not a mystery and the symbolism should be interpreted.

11 He that is unjust (not justified), let him be unjust still: and he which is filthy, let him be filthy still: and he that is righteous (by Christ), let him be righteous

still: and he that is holy, let him be holy still. (Daniel 12:9-13)

12 And, behold, I come quickly; and my reward is with me, to give to every man according as his work shall be.

By your unrighteous works, or by righteous faith in Jesus.

13 I am Alpha and Omega, the beginning and the end, the first and the last.

14 Blessed are they that do his commandments, (by faith) that they may have right to the tree of life, and may enter in through the gates into the city.

15 For without (the city of God) are dogs, and sorcerers, and whoremongers, and murderers, and idolaters, and whosoever loveth and maketh a lie.

This is God's eternal kingdom the holy city, and outside are the wicked, forever.

16 I Jesus have sent mine angel to testify unto you these things in the churches. (assemblies) I am the root and the offspring of David, and the bright and morning star.

The Sun of righteousness

17 And the Spirit, and the bride say, Come. And let him that heareth say, Come. And let him that is athirst come. And whosoever will, let him take the water of life freely.

18 For I testify unto every man that heareth the words of the prophecy of this book, If any man shall add unto

these things, God shall add unto him the plagues that are written in this book.

19 And if any man shall take away from the words of the book of this prophecy, God shall take away his part out of the book of life, and out of the holy city, and from the things which are written in this book:

20 He which testifieth these things saith, surely, I come quickly. Amen. Even so, come, Lord Jesus.

21 The grace of our Lord Jesus Christ be with you all. Amen

What is our relationship with Christ?

If you are a born-again believer, you can be confident in your relationship with him because he is faithful.

1 John 1:9 and 2:1-2 and read 2:12-14

> 1:9 If we confess our sins, he is faithful and just to forgive us our sins, and to cleans us from all unrighteousness.

> 1 John 2:1: My little children, these things write I unto you, that ye sin not. And if any man sin, we have an advocate with the Father, Jesus Christ the righteous: 2 And he is the propitiation for our sins: and not for ours only, but also for the sins of the whole world.

If you are a child of God you know it, or should. Matthew 16:13-20 Jesus asks, "Whom do men say that I the Son of man am?"

> 14 And they said, Some say that thou art John the Baptist: some, (Elijah) El-li'as; and others, Jeremias, or one of the prophets.

> 15 He saith unto them, But whom say ye that I am?

> 16 And Simon Peter answered and said, Thou art the Christ, (Messiah) the Son of the living God.

> 17 And Jesus answered and said unto him, Blessed art thou, Simon Bar-jon'a: for flesh and blood hath not revealed it unto thee, but my Father, which is in heaven. (revealed it to you)

> 18 And I say also unto thee, that thou art Peter, and upon this rock (this revelation) I will build my church; and the gates of hell shall not prevail against it.

The church is built on our faith in the death, burial, and resurrection of Jesus he is our foundation, not Peter, Peter was just a man. In fact, Jesus is the rock and the chief cornerstone of our faith.

> 19 And I will give unto thee the keys of the kingdom of heaven: and whatsoever thou shalt bind on earth shall be bound in heaven: and whatsoever thou shall loose on earth shall be loosed in heaven.

This is a lot of authority and it's not just for Peter. The promise is for all of us who believe.

> 20 Then charged he his disciples that they should tell no man that he was Jesus the Christ.

Why would Jesus tell them not to tell anybody that he was the Messiah? Because you must come to Jesus by faith, and all of Israel was looking for a king not necessarily a savior.

That is what Simon Peter did as a man of faith when he said thou art the Christ, the Son of the living God.

And the same blessing is for all who trust in the Lord. Are you ever concerned that you may have missed something or that you are not good enough?

Are you concerned that you might not make it into heaven?

I have heard many preachers teach that the parable of the ten virgins is the church, five good Christians and five bad but that's not the truth. We have been made righteous by our faith in the fact that Jesus bore our sins on the cross, we can't add anything to his grace.

So the story of the ten virgins is in the study of the parable in Matthew 25:1-13 which follows chapter 24 all the way from verse three where Jesus answered his disciples' question about the sign of his return and the end of the age (world).

Matthew 25

> 1 Then (at that time) shall the kingdom of heaven be likened unto ten virgins, who took their lamps, and went forth to meet the bridegroom.

The ten virgins "went forth" on their journey to meet the Lord.

> 2 And five of them were wise, and five were foolish.

> 3 They that were foolish took their lamps and took no (extra) oil with them.

The ten virgins must be on a journey, for some "took" no extra oil with them.

> 4 But the wise took oil in their vessels (their own bodies) with their lamps.

See 1 Thessalonians 4:4: That every one of you should know how to possess his vessel (body) in sanctification and honour;

The interpretation of the parable is this: The bridegroom is Jesus, and the virgins represent the world at the time of Jesus's return for his bride at the rapture of the church.

Again, the set up begins in Matthew Chapter 24:3 where Jesus describes the end of the age and the judgment to come and continues through Chapter 25. The virgins are the people of the earth.

The bridegroom takes only one wife, the bride of Christ who is the true church.

If you are a believer, you are the bride of Christ already and you are going with the bridegroom Jesus at his coming to take his bride to the marriage supper.

2 Corinthians 11:2: For I am jealous over you with a godly jealousy: for I have espoused you to one husband that I may present you as a chaste virgin to Christ.

The five wise virgins have already received Jesus in their hearts, the five foolish have put off a commitment to Jesus.

The Bible says that every man has been given the measure of faith so everyone has some oil in their lamp. Romans 12:3 God hath dealt to every man the measure of faith.

The extra oil that the wise have in their vessels, their own bodies is the anointing of the Holy Spirit which is a gift of salvation.

Matthew 25 continues

> 6 And at midnight (in the last moment) there was a cry made, Behold the bride groom cometh; go ye out to meet him.

The virgins must have started their trip in the dark and stopped at Motel 6 before midnight. In fact, the ten virgins represent the people of the world—all who start out in the dark on a journey seeking the light.

> 7 Then all those virgins arose, and trimmed their lamps.

> 8 and the foolish said unto the wise, Give us of your oil; for our lamps are gone out.

The foolish had not received the Holy Spirit, and the time of the rapture was at hand.

> 9 But the wise answered, saying, Not so; lest there be not enough for us and you: but go ye rather to them that sell, and buy for yourselves.

What does it mean to go and buy? In Revelation 3:18, Jesus said to the assembly in Laodicea: I counsel thee to buy of me gold tried in the fire (purified by his perfection), that thou mayest be rich; and white raiment (His righteousness), that thou mayest be clothed, and anoint your eyes with salve (of his Spirit), that you might see.

No one can buy righteousness or salvation; it is the gift of God to all who will receive it by faith in him and his righteousness.

> 10 And while they went out to buy, the bridegroom came; and they that were ready (the bride) went in with him to the marriage: and the door was shut.

Where are you going to buy oil at midnight? The appointed time of the church is over.

> 11 Afterward (after the rapture) came also the other virgins, saying, Lord, Lord, open to us.

God's grace is never ending but he cannot open the door again until the appointed time of the tribulation is complete.

> 12 But he answered and said, Verily I say unto you, I know you not.

When he comes for his church, or his bride, he takes his body of believers and shuts the door. If anyone thinks that the church is going into the tribulation, that person doesn't understand the scriptures.

> 13 Watch therefore, for ye know neither the day nor the hour wherein the Son of man cometh.

What is the meaning of the seven seals?

The seven seals can only be opened by the person with the authority to open the book. The scroll or book has writing on the front and back like modern books do today, but obviously the book is rolled like a scroll.

When Jesus opens the seals, he doesn't read the words written in the book. Perhaps that's why some people think the symbols of horsemen seen with the opening of the first four seals represent individual judgments.

But that is not consistent with the text. Read the opening of the fifth, sixth, and seventh seals again.

The fifth seal depicts God's tribulation saints having been killed. Would God bring judgment of death on his saints when his wrath is meant for the wicked?

The sixth seal depicts the battle of Armageddon Will God judge the wicked at Armageddon twice, once at the start and again at the end of this seven-year tribulation?

The seventh seal depicts a gap in time. Is judgment stated or implied?

Jesus has been given the authority to open the seals and to redeem his creation. Revelation 5:2 Says, "Who is worthy to open the book, and to loose the seals thereof?" Then in verse 5, Behold, the Lion of the tribe of Judah, the Root of David, hath prevailed to open the book, and loose the seven seals thereof.

> Revelation 5:9 Thou art worthy to take the book, and to open the seals thereof: for thou wast slain, and hast redeemed us to God by thy blood out of every kindred, and tongue, and people, and nation;
>
> 10 And hast made us unto our God kings and priests: to serve our God, and we shall reign on earth.

These verses are all about Jesus taking back his people, creation and his authority to rule with his people as the family of God.

Is the rapture relevant?

The day of the Lord, which lasts for roughly a thousand years, begins with the rapture of the church. The word rapture is the English translation of the Latin word *harpazo*, to snatch or catch away.

The day of the Lord should be divided into sections: The conclusion of the church age at the resurrection and rapture of his saints; then the tribulation judgments and the day of wrath at Armageddon which concludes the seventieth week of Daniel; and the time of Jacob's trouble.

Then his one-thousand-year rein on earth concludes with eternal judgment of the spiritually dead and reward to those whose life is in Christ.

And then the renewal of heaven and earth and his bringing heaven to earth.

The Day of the Lord is the judgment of the great day or great and terrible day or the great supper of the Lord which is Armageddon and the war of Gog and Magog.

But the Day of the Lord is also the whole time period from the rapture in Chapter 7 to the new Jerusalem in chapter 22.

2 Peter 3:8-9 and 15-16 But, beloved, be not ignorant of this one thing, that one day is with the Lord as a thousand years, and a thousand years as one day.

The apostles and the early church fully expected him to return for them at any moment.

Verse 9 The Lord is not slack concerning his promise, as some men count slackness; but is longsuffering (patient) to us-ward, not willing that any should perish, but that (giving time) all should come to repentance. Verses 15-16: even as … Paul also in all his epistles, speaking in them of these things; …

Concerning the rapture, we see in 1 Thessalonians 4:17: Then we which are alive and remain (at his appearing) shall be caught up together with them in the clouds to meet the Lord in the air: so shall we ever be with the Lord.

Why do we need to be snatched out of this world?

For one, the prophesy of Isaiah 13:9: Behold, the day of the LORD cometh, cruel both with wrath and fierce anger, to lay the land desolate: and he shall destroy the sinners thereof out of it.

All those who have not put their trust in Messiah Jesus are subject to God's wrath but the ones who do come to faith are subject to the wrath of Satan and the demons of hell.

Matthew 24:37-42 reads in part,

> 37 But as in the days of Noe (Noah) were, so shall the coming of the Son of man be.
>
> 38 For as in the days that were before the flood they were eating and drinking, marrying and giving in marriage, until the day that No'e (Noah) entered into the ark.
>
> 39 And (they) knew not until the flood came, and took them all away; so shall also the coming of the Son of man be.

Before the flood, the world was doing its own thing until Noah entered the ark and was caught up and carried above the judgment to safety.

They who ignored the warning were caught in the flood even though they had heard the judgment was coming, they ignored the warning and missed the boat.

Jesus, however, didn't leave those people in Hades. 1 Peter 3:19-20

> 19 By which also he went (in his Spirit) and preached unto the spirits in prison:
>
> 20 Which sometime were disobedient, when once the long suffering (patience) of God waited in the days of Noah, while the ark was a preparing …

Before the law there was no law, the people who died in the flood were given the opportunity to repent in Hades. No such opportunity is forthcoming.

Today the message of the rapture is well known but rejected even by many Christians. The message of the rapture should give us comfort and hope and inspire us to share the gospel of Jesus.

Back to Matthew 24

> 40 Then shall two be in the field; the one shall be taken (rapture), and the other left.

> 41 Two women shall be grinding at the mill; the one shall be taken and the other left.

Or they could be five virgins taken, and five virgins left behind.

> 42 Watch therefore: for ye know not what hour your Lord doth come (appear).

Matthew 24 3-36: Jesus is speaking of Jews in the time of tribulation not the church.

In verse 37, Jesus transitions to his pre-tribulation coming in the sky and is speaking about the rapture of the church and the consequences of not being ready for this event.

The first two verses of chapter 24 are often misunderstood so let's have a look at the context.

Matthew 24:1-2

> 1 And Jesus went out and departed from the temple: and his disciples came to him to shew him the buildings of the temple.

> 2 And Jesus said unto them, see ye not all these things? verily I say to you, There shall not be left here (at the temple) one stone left upon another, that shall not be thrown down.

The fall of Jerusalem and the destruction of the temple happened in 70 AD.

Okay so that was at the temple. I don't know how long Jesus and the disciples walked to get there, and I don't know how long they had been there, but Jesus was sitting on the Mount of Olives and his disciples came to him in private and asked him the following.

Matthew 24:3

> 3 And as he sat upon the Mount of Olives, the disciples came unto him privately, saying, tell us, when shall these things be? And what shall be the sign of thy coming, and the end of the world?

In verses 4 through 36, Jesus answers them with a prophesy to Jews concerning Israel, the descendants of Jacob, up to the time of Armageddon.

These scriptures in Matthew 24 and 25 are not about the destruction of the temple in Jerusalem.

Matthew 24:15 and 21, When ye therefore, shall see the abomination of desolation, spoken of by Daniel the prophet, stand in the holy place ...

This did not happen in AD 70.

Verse 21: For then shall be great tribulation, such as was not since the beginning of the world to this time, no, nor ever shall be.

Great tribulation is a onetime event.

Enoch was raptured. Genesis 5:24 And Enoch walked with God: and he was not; for God took him.

Elijah was raptured. 2 Kings 2:11 Elijah went up by a whirlwind into heaven.

So, is the rapture relevant? If you were to die today, would you go to be with Jesus?

If the rapture were to happen right now, would you go with him?

If you don't have a personal relationship with Jesus at his coming, or your leaving, the result will be tragic.

During the tribulation, will there be a temple in Jerusalem?

Again, speaking of the tribulation Jesus said in Matthew 24:15: When ye therefore, shall see the abomination of desolation, spoken of by Daniel the prophet, stand in the holy place whoso readeth, let him understand:

The holy place is the temple in Jerusalem Revelation Chapter 11:1-2 and Ezekiel Chapter 40.

So, there must be a temple in Jerusalem during the tribulation, Ezekiel, Daniel, Jesus, and John said there would be a temple, so who are you going to believe?

Will we live forever in heaven?

From the following scriptures we see that the Lord will restore the earth to its original state of perfection as he created it, and he will bring heaven down to earth so that he and we will live on earth forever.

Revelation Chapter 21:1-3 and 10

> 1 And I saw a new heaven and a new earth: for the first heaven and the first earth were passed away, and there was no more sea (ocean).

Isiah 11:15 says, And the Lord shall utterly destroy the tongue of the Egyptian sea; and with mighty wind shall he shake his hand over the river, and shall smite it in the seven streams, and make men go over dryshod (so that men can cross over in sandals or without getting wet).

Why a new heaven?

God's heaven, the third heaven, was never corrupted, but the first heaven, our atmosphere, and the second heaven, the stellar heavens were.

We have pictures of the moon and Mars showing dry lakes and riverbeds, and they will be restored. The earth will be restored, and there will be room for a lot more people. In fact, all of God's creation will be restored, and I would expect to see dinosaurs.

Outer space, the heavens and the galaxies, go on forever because God is eternal and his creation is eternal and it shall be inhabited, but God's home will be in the earth.

Revelation 21:2-3 and 10

> 2 And I, John, saw the holy city, new Jerusalem, coming down from God out of heaven, prepared as a bride adorned for her husband.
>
> 3 And I heard a great voice out of heaven saying, Behold, the tabernacle of God is with men, and he will dwell with them, and be their God.
>
> 10 And he carried me away in the Spirit to a great and high mountain, and shewed me that great city, the holy Jerusalem, descending out of heaven from God.

Isaiah 11:6-10

> 6 The wolf also shall dwell with the lamb, and the leopard shall lie down with the kid; and the calf and

> the young lion and the fatling together, and a little child shall lead them. Children will be born throughout eternity.

> 7 and the cow and the bear shall feed; their young ones shall lie down together. And the lion shall eat straw like the ox.

> As they were meant to from the time of creation.

> 8 And the nursing child shall play on the hole of the asp, and the weaned child shall put his hand on the adder's den (snakes' dens).

> 9 They shall not hurt or destroy in all my holy mountain (Kingdom): for the earth shall be full of the knowledge of the Lord, as the waters cover the sea.

There will be seas like the Sea of Galilee or perhaps even like the Great Lakes but no great oceans. This leaves plenty of room for whales.

> 10 And in that day there shall be a root of Jesse (Jesus), who shall stand for an ensign of the people; to him shall the nations seek, and his rest shall be glorious.

AUTHOR'S NOTE:

The Apocalypse, Rightly Dividing the Revelation is meant to be a study guide through the Book of Revelation.

I have included what I consider some misunderstood passages from other books of the Bible partly to make them clear and in part because they support The Apocalypse, or the Revelation of Jesus Christ to John.

I have laid out the context of the text in Revelation chronologically. If you are willing to take the time and employ the tools, this book will help you understand the Revelation.

You decide.

ABOUT THE AUTHOR

Mike Sanchez is from a farm and ranch background in the Four Corners area of Colorado and New Mexico.

He is a Christian with a deep abiding love for prophesy and the Book of Revelation in particular.

With no letters behind his name and no claim to fame, still he brings years of Bible study to light in this study of the Book of the Revelation of Jesus Christ.